a long WALK in the AUSTRALIAN BUSH

D1601435

a long

to Carlotta

WALK in the AUSTRALIAN BUSH

A15015 524440

GF
801
.L53
1998
West

William J. Lines

The University of Georgia Press
Athens

Published by the University of Georgia Press
Athens, Georgia 30602

© 1998 by William J. Lines

All rights reserved.

Designed by Di Quick.

Printed in Singapore.
02 01 00 99 98 P 5 4 3 2 1

Library of Congress Cataloging in Publication Data is available.

Contents

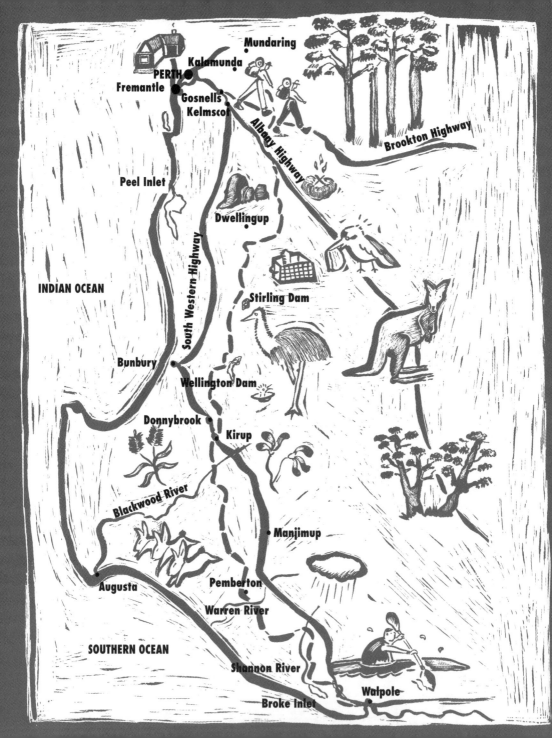

1

A first step begins

'It's boring!' a friend cautioned us. Our friend had trekked in the Himalayas, hiked in the Andes, watched the sun rise over the ruins at Machu Picchu, climbed Half Dome in Yosemite, rafted the Tatshenshini River in British Columbia and dived on the Great Barrier Reef. She had also walked sections of the Bibbulmun, a 650-kilometre track through the jarrah and karri forests of southwest Australia. In comparison ... well, there was no comparison. The Bibbulmun offered no grand vistas, no thundering waterfalls, no endless herds of wild animals migrating across vast wilderness, no monuments to ancient human effort. The Bibbulmun was domestic, familiar, uninteresting, boring.

Nevertheless, my companion, Carol, and I were not discouraged. We were determined to walk the track. We did not expect high drama or plan to scale great peaks or get caught up in a torrent of movement and stimulation. We wanted simply to walk, to listen, to look, to breathe, to be in the bush.

2

Our walk began early on the morning of 2 September 1993. We had spent the week with friends in Fremantle, where we bought provisions, packed and made plans for the five weeks we estimated we would be walking. This morning, stoked with anticipation, we were on our way. We went quietly downstairs, laced our walking boots and shouldered our packs.

The pale light of dawn spread across the sky as we waited in the cool air for a few minutes by Stirling Highway for the bus to Perth. In the city we transferred to a bus to Kalamunda, on the Darling Scarp, and the northern start of the Bibbulmun. Steadily, we made our way through the sandy, sprawling suburbs east of Perth.

Soon we were among the outskirts of the ever expanding, always growing suburbia. Houses alternated with open space, where grass, very little of it native, grew in the paddocks. Nor were the colours Australian. Bright morning sun highlighted tinges of blue encased in the early spring buds of Paterson's curse from North Africa and illuminated weeds from South Africa: brilliant yellow soursob, ochre capeweed, white, orange and pink watsonias, orange-red Cape tulips, white *Hersperantha falcata*, and patches of mauve and violet baboon flowers.

Just a few decades ago the paddocks grazed cows, sheep and chickens. Animal husbandry and home gardens once kept householders partly self-sufficient. Now, open space represents an indulgence—for people to graze horses before developers subdivide.

Before the land was cleared, fenced and turned into paddock, there was bush. These transformations reminded me that Carol and I were not about to embark on a trek through untouched wilderness. Not that I needed reminding. I had grown up here, on the coastal plain below the Darling Scarp, among the western margins of the once great jarrah forest. I had biked, walked barefoot and explored much of the country— orchards, quarries, reservoirs and bush—between Gosnells, Roleystone and Kalamunda. Those wanderings had familiarised me with a tamed and diminished country and had given me the feeling that the forest I knew was but a remnant of an older and much more enduring forest. Previous and present generations had torn out many of the first leaves and passages of that forest, mutilating it in many places.

Today, the forests not only *look* different from what the Aborigines knew and the first European settlers found—they *are* different. The annihilation of old growth, invasion by pests and diseases, contamination of surface and underground water sources by toxins and salt, punctuation by roads, clearcuts and mines, a decline in diversity of all types of plants and animals, and superintendence by an agency, the Western Australian Department of Conservation and Land Management (CALM), intent on the forest's destruction, are not merely signs of mistakes in the application of logging methods or management; they are evidence that those methods are inherently destructive and self-limiting.

Western Australians' relationship to the jarrah and karri forests is a paradigm of humanity's relationship to Earth. For in the jarrah and karri forests, Western Australians have had their way in almost everything. Politicians, loggers and developers dreamed of fertility, productivity and enrichment. The forests have, almost without resistance, given every gift. Likewise, on millions of hectares of destroyed forest across Australia and over the plundered planet, modern humans have worked out the logic of their technology, their religion, their moral beliefs, their social and economic priorities and their appetites.

Australians have transformed the continent so rapidly and extensively that the land has never had a chance to become a home. Australians have lived and continue to live in the future and so cannot possibly respect or even notice the present. The jarrah and karri forests exist only to be exploited for that future.

There is no mystery as to the cause of the deteriorating planet. The reasons are straightforward: an inherently destructive way of life that produces, consumes and wastes more than the earth can provide. The solutions are equally clear, although unacceptable to most. Repudiation of the solutions leads to a denial of the deterioration. In response, politicians and the people who rationalise destruction—scientists and those who control education, media and most civic institutions—call for more research. Research buys time and seeks means to avoid altering destructive habits. Optimists, informed by an ill-founded faith in science, assure us that ways will be found to manipulate nature to make the planet accommodate yet more humans and more destructive patterns of life. The ways of life responsible for destruction must themselves never be challenged; only their consequences might be mitigated.

Carol and I had seen destruction of the natural world wherever we had travelled. We were particularly aware of it in Carol's home country, the United States. But while destruction was familiar, hiking in the bush for such an extended period was not. The walk was doubly new for Carol: she had never hiked or walked in the Western Australian bush.

Our bus stopped in the centre of Kalamunda village. We bought pies and buns from a barkery and ate them on the steps of a stone church across from the sign marking the start of the track.

We felt elated, crossed the road and took a photograph of the sign. We started walking. Within 50 metres we were lost. The bush track ended abruptly at a road in the middle of a suburban development. We turned right and left but could not find the trail signs—yellow metal triangles, marked with a black snake symbol, the Waugal.

The Nyungar, the indigenous people of the southwest, knew the Waugal as the incarnation of the Korrndon Marma man, the creator. The Waugal inhabited deep pools, hills, valleys, rock outcrops and landmarks throughout the southwest. He watched over food laws and other laws and punished those who transgressed them. Wherever the Waugal travelled, he made a river. He made all the big rivers of the southwest. His camping places on these travels were sacred and known by the presence of lime, his excreta. Certain saltpans found in inland districts were formed from his urine.[1]

But, as obvious as the Waugal may have been to the Nyungar, it was invisible to us. We made several wrong turns before Carol asked directions from a mother taking her young children to kindergarten. She turned us around: the Waugals reappeared, nailed to trees along Spring Road, lined with new brick houses. The end of the road led to the real bush start of the Bibbulmun, in Kalamunda Conservation Area.

The track led east, north and southeast, and several times crossed a stream, a tributary of the Helena River. The ground was rocky and uneven. Our boots felt tight and unfamiliar, our steps heavy and our feet pinched. But the sky was clear and blue, the sun warm and the air was loaded with the sweet scent of honeybush (*Hakea lissocarpha*), its white and yellow flowers covering thick, prickly bushes growing along the banks of the trickling stream.

Many other flowers grew along the stream and up the stream banks. Most were familiar to me from my youthful rambles through the bush. The difference was that now I knew their names, impressed on my mind during the research and writing of my book *An All Consuming Passion*, about pioneer Western Australian botanist and bush lover Georgiana Molloy.

After an hour and a half the path climbed out of the stream valley and tended southeast, away from the Darling Scarp and into dry jarrah forest. Soon we were walking on the loose gravel of an old logging road. Several sections were steep and exposed. The air was dry and the sun shone hot on our backs. We started to sweat. Other sections passed through deep shade, on southern sides of hills, and were cool and moist.

Our packs grew very heavy very quickly. We cinched and tugged straps to adjust the weight and relieve our shoulders. But the adjustments merely left us agreeing that we carried too much weight. Because I carried the tent, stove and extra food, my pack weighed more than 20 kilograms, while Carol's was about 16 kilograms. These weights were relatively light considering the length and duration of the walk, but from years of hiking we had learned to keep our pack weights down. We would rather go hungry than carry heavy loads. We started listing the items to shed when we reached Dwellingup.

In planning the trip, we had divided the route into four sections of about eight to ten days' walk each: Kalamunda–Dwellingup, Dwellingup–Kirup, Kirup–Northcliffe, Northcliffe–Walpole. To post offices in Dwellingup, Kirup and Northcliffe we had mailed ourselves a parcel of supplies that contained enough food to take us through the next section. The first part of the walk took us through jarrah forest.

Jarrah (*Eucalyptus marginata*) is indigenous to Western Australia and grows within an area of about 6.4 million hectares, more or less continuously west of a line from New Norcia, Northam, York, Dryandra, Williams and Cranbrook to the coast. Isolated jarrah trees once grew throughout the uncleared wheat belt east of the boundary. A small group (since destroyed) grew 400 kilometres east of the boundary near Jilikin Rock and Mt Lesueur. These wheat belt populations indicate a much wider distribution of jarrah in a wetter past.

In more recent times the area where jarrah forest predominated covered about 3.9 million hectares. Prime jarrah forest, where jarrah grew in nearly pure stands, covered about 1.6 million hectares in a roughly compact block, 400 kilometres in length and about 40 kilometres in width, along the Darling Range. Here annual rainfall exceeds 1100 millimetres. The Bibbulmun passes through much of the length of this block.

Jarrah has red-brown, stringy bark with long vertical furrows. Mature trees average 27–37 metres in height, although they can grow to over 45 metres. Some trees have reached more than 50 metres in height, with diameters of 90–150 centimetres.

A few eucalypts grow in association with jarrah: marri (*E. calophylla*), wandoo (*E. wandoo*) and blackbutt (*E. patens*). But jarrah is dominant, owing, in part, to its greater resistance to fire than the other eucalypt species. Its thick bark insulates underlying live tissue from damage. Intense fires may kill leaves, twigs and branches, but the crown regenerates quickly from epicormic (dormant) buds on undamaged branches and trunks. Fire may also destroy seedlings and saplings, but these regenerate from below-ground lignotubers. Despite frequent fires jarrah trees can grow for a very long time. Trees repeatedly resprout from an original rootstock that may be as much as 7 metres across and many thousands of years old. Under natural conditions a jarrah forest is remarkably resilient. Under human management the forest faces multiple threats of destruction.

Perhaps the most remarkable fact about the jarrah forest is that it exists at all. Nowhere else in the world does a tall hardwood forest grow under such harsh climatic and inhospitable soil conditions. Yet jarrah thrives, along with a great diversity of plants and animals.

There are about 850 known flowering plant species in the jarrah forest. This specific diversity exists within the context of an even wider general diversity. The southwest of Western Australia is one of the world's richest botanical provinces. The area contains more than 6000 plant species, and more than 4000 of these are endemic. Such diversity persists despite the area's leached and impoverished soils. In fact, infertile soils may contribute to diversity. Primarily, however, diversity has probably arisen from a combination of stable geology, stable climate and drought.

Past glaciation and past droughts isolated the southwest from the rest of Australia. Drought created disjointed precincts, small patches of suitable soil and climate well separated from one another by inhospitable drought-prone country. Plants that were widespread during the warm-wet interglacial periods later became isolated in many islandlike populations. Within the isolated populations stable geology and stable climate favoured an orderly succession of plant changes. Populations evolved into separate species, even on deteriorating soils, which, in fact, provided further special habitats that allowed plants to persist and diversify.

All the jarrah forest that Carol and I passed through on our first day on the Bibbulmun had been cut-over at least once. Immense stumps and logs remained, reminders of a once very different forest, dominated by well-spaced but large trees that towered over and blocked the sunlight to a patchy undergrowth. Early settlers riding through the original jarrah forest described it as being like a deer park. But logging has destroyed the tall, light-blocking canopy and opened the forest to a dense growth of ground vegetation and young trees.

Nineteenth-century and early-twentieth-century loggers felled the whole tree but took only the bole, that part of the trunk up to the first branch. They left the rest where it fell. Big logs have survived the many fires that have swept the area since the first fellings, and they lie intact on the forest floor. They served as seats beside the path when we wanted to rest.

Off to the side of the track we saw two men chainsawing old fallen timber and loading firewood into their truck. On the track, coming the opposite way, a hiker carried a bike over his shoulders. A young Canadian who was staying at the Mundaring Youth Hostel, he had decided to do a day circuit of a part of the track. He thought he might return and attempt the whole Bibbulmun by bike next autumn.

Carol and I walked on and soon reached Pickering Brook, once a tributary of the Helena River. Its waters now flow directly into Helena River Reservoir, behind Mundaring Weir. The reservoir, which supplies water to the eastern goldfields, is the most northerly of the large, state-owned water-supply reservoirs in the Darling Range. In total, these reservoirs have inundated more than 8000 hectares of river valley.[2]

At Pickering Brook we stood before a great swath of cleared land underneath high voltage power lines carried on large steel towers. A unit of army motorcyclists roared by on the inspection track. They passed us without so much as a nod. I stepped down to the brook near a culvert and filled our canteens.

After another hour's walk we decided to camp. Although the site was without water, we felt we had gone far enough for one day. We pitched the tent in the middle of a side road, set the stove on a stump and cooked our first Bibbulmun meal.

The sun set and shadows lengthened. We talked about the day's hike and looked at the map of tomorrow's route. Stars appeared, precise and bright. I pointed out the Southern Cross to Carol and hoped that it would become an ever fixed point for her. As the earth revolved eastward and the sun sank farther below the western horizon, the Milky Way, directly overhead, became more brilliant. The sky then began to pale. To the east, at ground level, around the dark forms of silhouetted trees, a bright and mysterious light appeared. Fellow campers? Or perhaps it was an electric light from a farm.

With the puzzle unsolved we prepared for bed. As Carol burrowed into the tent, I suddenly realised the light's source: the rising full moon.

We felt like fools. Relieved by the explanation, Carol decided to stay up to watch the great golden orb rise above the trees.

We slept well and woke at first light. My muscles were much less sore and stiff than I had expected, but I did have blisters on my feet.

Nevertheless, we covered the first few kilometres in good time and rested by pretty Little Darkin River, which, like Pickering Brook, empties into Helena River Reservoir. We splashed our faces, filled our canteens and had a snack. For 50 metres on either side of the stream jarrah gave way to a border of white-barked wandoo.

The track, still tending southeast, now climbed out of the stream valley along Darkin Ridge Road. We heard rustling in the undergrowth. A family of wild black pigs—two adults and four piglets—appeared, running parallel to the road. Once ahead of us they galloped across the road and disappeared into the bush on the other side.

Most of the day's walk was uphill and our packs began to bear heavily on our shoulders and backs. I felt I had never carried a heavier load. Certainly I had never before carried ten days' worth of food. But the weight on my back was tolerable compared to the crippling effect of my boots on my feet. The constant pain distracted me from enjoying the walk. The walk was beginning to tell on Carol as well. Most of the day's walk was uphill. She found her pack very heavy and felt the strain.

Breaks afforded temporary relief, but when we resumed walking we could hardly put one foot ahead of the other. We felt stiff and burdened. Only an effort of will enabled us to take the first step after a rest.

But we kept walking, and I could sense that somewhere beyond the heavy pack, aching joints and blistered feet lay the possibility of a rhythm to our trek. This would be found only when we had walked long enough so that what we thought of was not urban life and the concerns of the human world but incidents along the track and scenery passed through.

All our thoughts and memories would then be focused on the bush and on our passage through the bush.

The more I accepted this possibility, the more I realised how, in the meantime, we, like most humans, were such fidgets, beset with all sorts of trivialities of a passing nature, buzzing in and out of our minds like flies. When we walked in rhythm, however, we would be utterly absorbed and content, resoved in a belief of walking without even thinking of an end or a purpose to walking.

Others had once derived such a cadence and an exuberance from life in the bush. Before the coming of the Europeans, a few thousand Aboriginal people had lived in the southwest. Possibly half the population, those who had occupied the western coastal plain, moved to the jarrah forest in the winter to avoid coastal winter storms.

Their use of the forest was minimal and much less intensive than on the coast. But the Nyungar ate everything edible, including acacia seeds, quandong nuts, Podocarpus fruits, young leaves of blackboys, zamia nuts—soaked for long periods to remove toxins—yam roots and fungi. These were eaten raw. Other foods were pounded and roasted on hot coals or heated stones. The forest also yielded kangaroos, possums, reptiles, birds, small mammals, fish, crustaceans and insects.

Since foraging quickly depleted local foods, winter camps were temporary, occupied for only a few days at a time. The Nyungar camped in valleys near rock holes, swamps, springs, creeks, or rivers and where the soil was sandy, for comfort. Few Nyungar were likely to stay in the forest in the summer. Because water was crucial and the forest was much drier at that time of year, people moved to the more permanent pools and lakes that were common on the coastal plain.

Neither the Nyungar nor any other Aboriginal group 'managed' their 'environment'. Aborigines had no word for and no concept of management, and they did not look upon the world around them as their environment. If a people lacked managerial notions like ours, then they simply did not have them, and it is gratuitous to suggest that, in spite of this, they engaged in 'managerial' activities and agendas paralleling our own. To call what Aborigines did in their encounters with the natural world 'management' prejudges and limits those encounters and carries misleading connotations about administration, regulation, control and progress that, although comforting to modern prejudices, do not reflect Aboriginal society.

In moving back and forth, the Nyungar took their time. They travelled leisurely. They did not lust after speed and felt no compulsion to make life faster. They understood that time was nothing if not measured, and that every plant, animal, stone, star, band and family group had its own unique measure of time. This measure demanded obedience to the rhythm of seasons and the great cycle of renewal, in which they themselves were intimate participants.

The Nyungar located themselves in relation to where their kinfolk were and where food and water were. Boundaries were adaptable. As wanderers, the Nyungar lived inclusive, flexible lives.

Unlike modern people, the Nyungar did not see the present as merely a step into the future, as an opportunity to change the world. They did not regard the forest as potential, as an object separate from themselves to be remade and transformed for the purposes of enrichment. Nor did they regard the past as a foreign country, remote from contemporary concerns. They viewed the past as ever present and as a persistent source of meaning and authority. For the Nyungar, past, present and future collapsed into an eternal now.

Recognising that they lived in a country vibrating with the unceasing renewal of all forms of life, the Nyungar called themselves and the land they lived in Bibbulmun. According to Daisy Bates, the term is a compound comprising the word *bib*, which means breasts, and *bul* or *bula*, which means many, plenty. Bates suggests that Bibbul—the singular term for Bibbulmun (the suffix *-mun* forming the plural)—means a people with many females among them. But Bates's interpretation is too clever. Since traditional people thought symbolically and figuratively—that is, poetically—it is more likely that Bibbulmun meant what it says: a people and a land of many breasts. Breasts represent fecundity and nourishment, and so the word *Bibbulmun* acknowledges a people blessed with plenty, living in a land of plenty.

But we will never know for certain. There are no native speakers of Nyungar left. When Bates placed her explanation for the derivation of Bibbulmun before members of the Nyungar, 'the reply in all cases was *kubbain* (it might be so, perhaps); no one could tell the origin of the name by which they were called; they were always Bibbulmun to themselves and to the tribes adjoining them.'[3]

2

Through a
forest undone

Almost all of the Bibbulmun walking track, 650 kilometres from Kalamunda to Walpole on the south coast, passes through land under CALM management. Designated a long-distance walking track in 1979, the Bibbulmun, for the most part, followed logging and fire roads. Track designers divided the route into stages and placed campsites approximately one day's walk apart (15–25 kilometres). Between Kalamunda and Dwellingup the track passes through water catchments. In order to avoid water contamination, each campsite in this section had a pit toilet and, usually, a water tank, filled by the run-off from the toilet roof.

On our second night in the forest, Carol and I camped at what CALM's publication *A Guide to the Bibbulmun Track* referred to with machine precision as stage 3A. Near Mt Dale, it lay to the right of the track on bare, grey sand under scattered and recently burned jarrah trees and blackboys (*Xanthorrhoea* sp.). After we pitched the tent, clouds appeared in the west and the wind picked up—signs of a rain-bearing front. We took up the tarp groundsheet, tied it to several blackboys and suspended it over the tent. We stored our packs under cover in the toilet.

The wind continued and rain started soon after we got into the tent. It rained throughout the night. The air inside the tent was hot, close and damp. We slept poorly and emerged in the morning stiff and drowsy. Our bedding and clothes were wet.

The drying of our gear delayed our departure and another shower kept us off the track. We were reluctant walkers anyway. Upon removing our boots the previous night, we had uncovered more blisters. Carol's feet were as raw as mine.

From stage 3A the track turned due south. We were as far east into the jarrah forest as we were ever to be. The track crossed wet, swampy heath and for a couple of kilometres followed the cleared right of way bulldozed through the bush under high voltage transmission lines. We crossed Brookton Highway and re-entered dry jarrah forest. Like all the forest we had so far passed through, the jarrah here had been cut over two or more times since the nineteenth century.

The exploitation of jarrah for timber began with the founding of the Swan River Colony in 1829. One of the ships in the first convoy, HMS *Sulphur*, was repaired with what the settlers referred to as 'Swan River mahogany'. The Nyungar term for the tree was *Djara*, subsequently anglicised and mispronounced as jarrah.

The British Admiralty was impressed with the repair work on HMS *Sulphur* and ordered 200 tons of Swan River mahogany in 1831. Another order from the Royal Naval Dockyards followed in 1837. Most of these trees were cut from around the settlements on the coastal plain. Tested in England, Swan River mahogany was found to be amazingly durable.

Over the next two decades the worldwide construction of railways brought a demand for sturdy railway sleepers cut from exceptionally strong and lasting timber able to withstand attack from rot and termites. Jarrah seemed ideal. But the first efforts at large-scale exploitation failed. Early mills were undercapitalised and short of labour.

In the 1850s local entrepreneur Benjamin Mason solved the labour problem by employing former convicts to cut timber at Bickley Brook, near Kalamunda. He hauled the timber by bullock to a wharf on the Canning River at Cannington and then lightered it down the Canning to the Swan River and on to the port of Fremantle. Double handling added greatly to costs, and Mason could barely compete against world timber prices.

Despite the difficulties, exports grew. Between 1850 and 1870 an average of 1400 cubic metres of timber was shipped annually from the Swan River Colony. In addition to railway sleepers for the eastern colonies of Australia, Great Britain, New Zealand, Mauritius, South Africa, Ceylon and China, local mills cut telegraph poles for newly erected lines in South Australia and jetty piles and wharfing timber for South America.

Until 1870 most logging took place on the margins of the main jarrah forest. Exploitation had barely begun, especially considering that everyone connected with the colony felt that the forest was ruinously underexploited. The settlers viewed the forest as inexhaustible in extent and inexhaustible in timber. When the Reverend John Ramsden Wollaston reached the forest at the Collie River in 1851, while on a journey from Albany to Perth, he described the jarrah as 'in inexhaustible abundance'.[1]

This was a convenient and necessary delusion, fostered by a colonial government that saw its main tasks as developing private enterprise and exploiting nature. Accordingly, it offered generous inducements to businessmen.

In 1870 Western Australian governor Frederick Weld granted timber concessions to three millers: 40 000 hectares to Benjamin Mason on the Canning River east of Kelmscott; 101 000 hectares to a syndicate from

Ballarat, the Rockingham Jarrah Timber Company Limited (whose partners included Eureka Stockade hero Peter Lalor) at Jarrahdale; and 81 000 hectares to a rival of Mason's, George Simpson, at Lockeville, near Busselton.

These companies industrialised logging with railway lines, steam locomotives, steam loaders and steam skidders. By 1878 six steam mills and three water mills operated in the forest. Industrialisation turned the forest into a wasteland of fallen and broken logs and piles of crushed and split branches. Slash was everywhere, piles of it drying. The inevitable happened: the build-up of logs and debris provided fuel for devastating fires, which swept through the forest in the 1870s. Much standing timber was destroyed. The newly bare ground was exposed to gully and sheet erosion. Erosion weakened the foundations for regrowth and clogged streams with sediment.

The Colonial Office in London grew concerned about the rapacity of exploitation and querried colonial practice. The Western Australian government assured the British government that, because of the illimitable extent of the forests, it was too early to think of conservation. Moreover, the timber concessions were a success. Between 1871 and 1882 timber exports grew in value over sixfold, from £15 300 to £93 650.

Botanist Baron Ferdinand von Mueller visited the southwest forests in 1867 and again in 1877. He concluded that the forests were not illimitable but predicted 'that *E. marginata* is destined to supply one of the most lasting of hardwood timbers for a long time to come, at the least costly rate, to very many parts of the globe'. Mueller was forward looking and modern. Anticipating twentieth-century obsessions with management and order, he recommended a bureaucratic structure for the rational control of the forests that would exercise 'surveillance over the existing timber resources of the State in order to prevent waste and to encourage, regulate and to protect the natural upgrowth of young trees'.[2]

Waste also disturbed the commissioner of Crown lands, Malcolm Fraser, who, in an 1882 report, recommended the appointment of an inspector of forests and timber stations to 'prevent as far as possible the great waste and destruction now going on in our Timber Forests'. He stressed, however, that since the untouched forest area was so large, 'no anxiety need be felt as to the exhaustion of supplies for many years.'[3]

In the meantime, logging accelerated. New syndicates formed, took over old concessions and expanded into new ones. A government railway line cut through the jarrah forest and further extended the reach of the timber companies. Exports increased. Between 1893 and 1900, 62 million jarrah blocks (923 centimetres by 8 centimetres) were exported through Rockingham for use on city streets in London, Paris, Glasgow and Melbourne.

Early in the new century, however, overseas demand for timber fell. Coincidentally, the local government building program slowed. Timber prices dropped. It was time, some politicians argued, for a royal commission.

The commission reported in 1904. It found that the area of cut-over jarrah comprised some 61 000 hectares; that the 813 000 hectares of remaining jarrah forest was suitable for milling; that, based on the then current rate of cutting of about 24 000 hectares a year, the forest would last another 32 years; and that hewing sleepers involved enormous waste.[4]

The report recommended the abolition of the lease system and its replacement by a royalty system. This effectively opened up more forest to the smaller sawmillers. Two of those millers, Arthur Bunning and the Whittaker brothers, Edwin and Arthur, took advantage of the new free-for-all and began to build their own forest empires.

Their growth, however, did not come at the expense of the largest miller. By 1909 Millars, founded by Charles and Edwin Millar in 1884, owned or controlled 610 000 hectares of forest land, 560 kilometres of railway, 40 locomotives, 800 wagons, more than 1000 horses, 26 sawmills and 3 shipping ports. The company employed 3500 men, produced 283 000 cubic metres of hardwood a year, and had offices and agencies throughout the world, with private shipping docks in Western Australia and on the Tilbury Docks, London, as well as timber depots in India, Ceylon, the Philippines, China, South Africa and New Zealand.

The government, urging still more exploitation, entered the industry in 1913 and opened three large mills. By the time of the outbreak of the Great War, there were 35 sawmills operating throughout the state, most of them in the jarrah forest. Almost all the high-quality stands of timber in the northern jarrah forest had now been destroyed.

Robert Robinson, the minister for industries and woods and forests, commented in 1918:

> Since 1836 Western Australia has been engaged in mining her forests, that is to say she has striven, regardless of the future, to get as much as she possibly could out of the areas of timber country that be scattered within her borders. Timber men have been encouraged to take up forests for saw-milling purposes, and the terms under which concessions have been granted were of the most advantageous character. The object of each successive Government has been to exploit as much timber as possible in the shortest time.[5]

Robinson's view of logging as mining had the virtue of honesty. It was free of self-deception, unlike the bureaucratic obfuscations that were to justify exploitation under later-twentieth-century management.[6]

Fortunately for our feet, our third day's hike was short—less than 13 kilometres. The designated campsite, however, stage 4A, Abyssinia Rock, actually lay 1.5 kilometres along a side road off the main track.

Abyssinia Rock was a popular camping area. Besides pit toilets and a water tank, CALM had supplied fire rings. These were stuffed with rubbish. All the campsites we had passed through so far had been strewn with rubbish. Rubbish also lay along the track. In the bush itself we saw many burned-out, rusting car bodies, discarded as thoughtlessly as they had been acquired. But Abyssinia Rock was the worst. Plastic and glass bottles, cans, jars, plastic wrap, paper and aluminium foil—tokens of the nation's intimacy with nature—spilled out of the fire pits, spread over the ground, lay entangled in bushes and wrapped around tree trunks.

We pitched our tent away from the fire pits. After the rainstorm of the night before, the skies had cleared and the day was sunny. We hung our wet gear to dry. While Carol rested in the tent, I walked through a low scrub of yellow-flowering wattle (*Acacia laperiticola*) and red-flowering prickly bitter-pea (*Daviesia decurrens*) to the flat expanse of Abyssinia Rock.

Granite outcrops are common in the jarrah forest and throughout the southwest. Some occur as domes, others as sheets with areas varying from a few square metres to a few hectares. Like all of them, Abyssinia Rock was very weathered, marked by fissures, ridges and depressions, and coloured black and green by moss and lichen. Other similarly hardy vegetation, able to tolerate great extremes—saturation in winter, scorching, dry heat in summer—grew here and there. Alpine-like flowers—mud mat, large blind grass and pincushions—grew in depressions where enough organic matter had accumulated to form a thin soil. Deeper depressions supported larger bushes: pink feather flower, red granite bottlebrush and hakea.

On the brown, gritty loam of the soil apron at the base of the rock, young stems of the elbow orchid (*Spiculaea ciliata*), common on and around granite outcrops from the Darling Scarp to the edge of the desert, were showing. The elbow orchid is one of a number of orchids unique to Western Australia. These plants dupe male wasps into pollinating their flowers. Part of the flower mimics the wingless female wasp and even emits the right sex-attracting scent. Male wasps alight on the flower, grab hold of the 'female' and try to fly off with it. But the flower is hinged so that the wasp swings upward and is neatly clasped with its back against the pollen and stigma. It then flies off, with pollen attached, to find its next mate.

On the sloping rock, great slabs of flaked stone lay against the rounded surface. Some of the smaller flakes had been picked up and thrown about but, given the rubbish in the nearby campground, Abyssinia Rock itself was relatively undisturbed. The whole formed an almost self-contained and delightful world of miniature flora.

There are few things worse while camping than cooking and eating in the dark. Carol and I planned each day's walk on the Bibbulmun so that we would arrive in camp with plenty of time to cook and eat before dark, which, because it was September, came early. Just as we were settling down to dinner at Abyssinia Rock, a troop of scouts, in straggling singles, pairs and groups—about twenty in all—wandered into the campsite, followed by three adults. Carol's spirits dived at the prospect of a night in such boisterous company. But, I said, better to have scouts for fellow campers than the vandals responsible for trashing the place.

When the adults arrived, they directed adolescent energy towards picking up the rubbish. After completing their good deed, the scouts paired off and began lighting fires. As darkness fell we were surrounded by flame. The scouts' fascination with fire, however, was brief. Soon the whole troop was in bed. The night was still.

Next morning we rose at dawn, broke camp and then ate porridge, our regular breakfast. In preparing breakfasts for the trip, we had filled ziplock bags with a cup of instant oats, raisins and instant milk powder. To cook, I emptied the contents into a pot, added water and brought the pot to a boil over the stove. Carol always boiled herself one cup of water for coffee, a beverage I do not drink..

Carol applied lotion to our blisters before bandaging them. To further alleviate pressure on our feet we readjusted the contents of our packs.

The country we now walked through had once been part of Benjamin Mason's timber lease. But the forest had been cut at least once more since Mason had finished with it. The narrow track, overgrown with regrowth scrub, continued nearly due south, very straight, very level and, considering that we were passing through a heathy swamp, very solid. We realised we were following an old railway bed that had once tethered this forest to the world. A couple of kilometres farther on, the Bibbulmun abruptly changed direction southwest. We left the swamp, climbed slightly through woodland, then descended to the headwaters of a branch of the Canning River.

The Canning River, like the Helena River, is part of the Swan River drainage basin. Most of its catchment lies in state forest. The river and three of its tributaries—Churchman Brook, Munday Brook and Wungong Brook—have been dammed to provide drinking water to Perth. Below the main dam the river has become eutrophic through nutrients leaching from bordering septic systems, golf courses, house gardens and market gardens. Both the Canning and the Swan Rivers, into which the Canning flows, blossom with algae—toxic blue-green algae in the Canning and 'red tide' dinoflagellates in the Swan.

We crossed several brooks, and the vegetation became lush, almost rainforest. The weather turned damp. We put on rain gear, sat on a large log, had a snack and breathed the cool, moist air. Our feet still hurt but we found the pain tolerable at last.

Early in the afternoon, after a hike of 18 kilometres, we reached campsite 5A, 100 metres off the track in the scrub. Rain fell as we surveyed the area, which, like Abyssinia Rock, contained a pit toilet, water tank and metal fire rings with plates. One ring had once been smothered by a fire so hot that the metal had been twisted out of shape. Overall, however, the site looked far less abused than the one at Abyssinia Rock. Following our criteria of level ground and proximity to trees or blackboys around which to tie the tarp cover, we selected a spot for the tent.

With the dead and dry fronds taken from the underskirt of a blackboy I started a fire, our first since we began the walk. We spent the afternoon making camp: gathering wood, tending the fire and heating water. Carol washed herself with a damp, soapy cloth.

We stayed up late, staring into the fire. I showed Carol how the addition of even a small branch of dried and volatile eucalyptus leaves produced a blazing flash of light. We watched the flames and sparks shoot upwards to the stars.

Some of the light from those stars had begun its journey towards the earth when Georgiana Molloy lived in the southwest. Some of the starlight studding the sky has been travelling through space at its fantastic speed far longer. When we look at the stars, we are looking into the past. Much of the light is the fossil remains of once blazing stars perhaps no longer shining, or changed into objects larger or smaller, brighter or dimmer, or of colour many hues different from the brilliant blues and reds and whites sprinkling the present sky.

'Where did it come from?' Carol asked. 'Where is it all going?'

With the tremendous authority Carol had learned to distrust, I gave the standard scientific explanations of the big bang, black holes, space–time, relativity, quantum theory and cosmology, the little picture and the big picture. None provided concrete answers, all was theory, conjecture, speculation and none addressed the greatest mystery, the biggest unknown: life on this lovely planet, Earth.

The sky clouded over. As we crawled into the tent, the first drops of rain fell. Rain continued throughout the night and was falling at first light. Fortunately, we had learned to hang the tarp so that it shed water well away from the tent. We were dry and we stayed dry. With showers continuing, we sheltered under the tarp as we folded the tent and packed the backpacks. Foolishly, I had left the stove out overnight. Now it was soaked and would not light. We left without eating breakfast.

A flock of black cockatoos screeched and called from far off trees as we walked down the sodden track. Successive showers swept down. Four kilometres from the camp the track climbed over Sullivan Rock, a large domelike granite outcrop, an island of rock in the surrounding sea of bush. Water streamed off the surface in dozens of rivulets. Like Abyssinia Rock, Sullivan Rock was covered in moss and lichen. Plants grew in the soil that had accumulated in shallow depressions, crevices and under ledges. We followed the path to Albany Highway. Trucks and cars sped by and threw up huge arching sheets of spray.

We crossed to a roadside pullout with picnic tables, set our gear down at a table and assembled the stove to cook porridge. As the mix came to a boil, rain started falling. A twenty-minute deluge followed. We ate quickly and sheltered under a large tree. When the shower passed, we started walking. Frequent rain marked the walk, but our ponchos kept us and out packs dry.

Since our camp at 3A we had been content to follow CALM's camping and walking recommendations. Today we set our goal as 6A, some 17 kilometres from 5A. Although not far from busy Albany Highway, 6A seemed the most remote and least trashed of all the campsites so far. The farther from Perth these sites were, the less rubbish they contained. Sites with easy access were littered with rubbish, whereas sites that required effort to reach were generally left as they had been found.

The trashing of the bush parallels the abusing of the planet. In both cases people do not understand what they are doing because they do not understand what they are undoing. Urbanity has corrupted perception, and most people are now urbanites. Characteristically, urbanites—whose experience of natural things is minimal—are unaware of and uninterested in the existence of the natural world. Cities, where everything has been formed for human purpose, detach people from nature. City dwellers are preoccupied with industry, property, sales, merchandising, getting and spending. They are likely to be indifferent, or even hostile, to anything that lies beyond commercial possibilities. The bush, indeed the whole living planet, exists as a plaything, a novelty, an object of profit and consumption. Nature's disposability arises from the urban belief in progress and modernity—ideas based more on erasing a sense of locale than of living in it. Nature itself has become a theme.

The disconnection between people and place also derives from modern notions of identity. Identity once referred to a sense of self based on a life history or narrative that took place in a durable physical world that outlasted individual life. The world most people now live in, a world of commodities and consumption, a world of ephemera and of constant innovation, requires perpetual self-reinvention and a boundless appetite for change. Accordingly, modern psychology and the human potential movement have redefined identity, linked it to a fluid, protean, 'socially constructed' problematical self, and eliminated the old association between identity and continuity. Identity floated free of place because people no longer inhabited a world that existed independently of themselves.[7]

Education reinforces this overwhelming nihilism and egoism. Modern education teaches children 'self-esteem' and 'self-expression'. Children learn that they can be and do anything they want and that the world belongs to them. They are inculcated with the idea of the primacy of individual desire. They are not taught that a true sense of self depends on realising the inevitable and tragic gap between expectation and fulfilment. The most valuable lesson children can learn is that all that lives must die.

3

By cankered soil
and strangled trees

Whenever humans plan destruction, they disguise their intentions in language. To destroy a forest, and to put an end to life, language must rule. To destroy, humans must first excoriate.

Western Australia's jarrah forest has been felled to the accompaniment of a litany of calumny against the forest (and its defenders) and justified with a catalogue of words (that disguise violence and rapacity) from the vocabularies of aesthetics, management, science and progress.

'Taken as a whole there is nothing particularly picturesque about the appearance of a jarrah tree or a forest of these. Indeed, the general effect of the species *en masse* is dull, sombre, and uninteresting to the eye,' wrote Western Australia's first conservator of forests, John Ednie-Brown, in 1896. Ednie-Brown was not just voicing an aesthetic judgment. His opinions had consequences. Ednie-Brown's priority lay in use and exploitation; an 'uninteresting' forest was simply easier to destroy.[1]

Ednie-Brown's successor, Charles Edward Lane-Poole, appointed inspector general of forests for Western Australia in 1916, also believed in use. Lane-Poole's language, however, derived from management and science and reflected an industrial view of the forest. He believed in efficiency. He regarded the natural world as an engineer would a problem. Production, and more production, should become the goal in the organisation of nature. For Lane-Poole the question of whether the forest was picturesque was irrelevant. He sought objective criteria and disguised destruction behind the circumlocution of 'sustained yield'.

Sustained yield meant a continuous supply of timber based on achieving a balance of timber harvests with growth. Foresters would determine how much annual net growth a particular forest area supported (overall growth minus death and decay) and then limit timber harvests to that annual 'growth increment', which was the sustainable yield of timber.

Conservation under sustained yield meant not preservation but a stable flow of commodities and enlargement of the human domain through greater use of the forest. The chief obstacle in the way of full use was waste. Current logging practices, Lane-Poole believed, were wasteful. 'There is no subject,' he wrote in 1920, 'more important in the economics of timber than research into timber waste . . . eighty percent of the tree is destroyed and lost and it is for the forest products laboratory to find uses for the various parts now wasted.'[2]

Since the nineteenth century, foresters have conducted an unceasing campaign against 'waste'. By waste they mean unused parts of the forest. Intolerance of waste reflects intolerance for any deviation from utilitarian values. The idea of waste is an adjunct to the ideology of wood production.

Environmentalists share this fear of waste and condemn waste with almost as much vehemence as professional foresters. But paranoia over waste serves to obscure what is really happening in the forest. Foresters pretend that the real crime in the forest is waste. Conservationists endorse this view when they too condemn waste. But the focus on waste disguises the real outrage: exploitation and destruction. Taking everything, reducing waste, is akin to strip mining the life of the forest.

In criticising loggers for wasteful harvesting practices, Lane-Poole was not criticising industrial forestry as such, but rather the failure of industry to practise what he considered a sustainable form of tree farming. After all, foresters and loggers shared a common outlook: forests were economic assets.

By the early decades of the century, the idea that forests were resources and forestry an industry was so commonplace and so innocuous that even royalty advocated it. In 1920 George V told the British Empire Forestry Conference in London: 'It is a peculiar difficulty of forestry that it demands perhaps more imagination, more patience, and more foresight than any other industry.'[3]

The people best able to provide these qualities, everyone at the conference agreed, were foresters. By 1920 every Australian state had established a forestry commission or department. In Western Australia, under Lane-Poole, the Forests Department introduced management into the forest: classification, inventory and working plans based on a cutting cycle of 30 years. Foresters marked trees to be felled and indicated their direction of fall.

Lane-Poole's management ideas, however, earned him the enmity and opposition of Millars and timber industry workers. They were not ready for twentieth-century euphemisms such as sustained yield. They preferred the old style, called a spade a spade, and called logging mining. In 1922 Lane-Poole resigned.

Falling and milling continued, reached a climax in 1926, diminished slightly over the next four years and practically ceased as the Depression deepened. By then, two-thirds of all the forest under the Forests Department's jurisdiction, including almost all the prime jarrah forest, had been cut over. But although logging slowed, the Forests Department did not. Under the guise of management, foresters were obsessively busy preparing the forest for a new round of exploitation. By the end of the Second World War the Forests Department had pushed nearly 18 000 kilometres of roads and firelines and more than 2000 kilometres of telephone wire through the forest.

Roads are biologically sterile and remain so for decades. Where they do support life—on their margins—they permit the ingress of exotic weeds. The new roads in the jarrah forest added up to thousands of hectares of sterility, pathways for disease and routes for invasion by weeds and feral animals. With the forest gridded with roads, a new cycle of logging and destruction was about to begin.[4]

On the sixth day of our walk, Carol and I noted, as we had most days, fresh kangaroo tracks. Several hopped through the adjacent bush. The route to 7A covered 15 kilometres. I enjoyed every step, even during the regular cloudbursts, including hail. I had finally found my stride; my feet were no longer blistered to distraction. I inhaled the bush, smelled the moisture and gloried in the vibrancy of wet foliage and the life-bringing water sheeting across the track.

The day's walk took us through the watershed of the Serpentine River. We crossed several tributaries, as well as the upper reaches of the Serpentine itself. Like most rivers in the jarrah forest the Serpentine is dammed. A large storage reservoir, with two arms each more than

10 kilometres long, and a pipehead dam that banks the water back nearly 5 kilometres have inundated long sections of riverside bush. The impounded water is pumped to Perth's growing, thirsty suburbs.

Below the dam, the river's flow has been greatly reduced and what remains has been tamed and confined within levee banks. Many of its associated wetlands have been drained. Loads of nutrients (principally phosphate), leached from surrounding farmland, flush into Peel Inlet, combine with nutrients brought in by other rivers and culminate in massive spring blooms of blue-green algae.

Eighty percent of the rivers in the southwest suffer from salinity, bank erosion and sedimentation, nutrient and toxin pollution, reduced flow, loss of riparian vegetation and invasion by exotic fauna and flora. Much of the degradation is irreversible and is likely to become worse. State water authorities plan more dams, more inundation and more management.

For a short while the Bibbulmun followed North East Road, a gazetted byway joining Albany Highway and Pinjarra. We saw no traffic. On leaving North East Road, the track followed the flat and nearly straight Nifty Formation. (The term *formation* refers to an old road or railway bed.)

As we walked south, the forest became noticeably wetter and lusher. Frogs croaked from the many streams, puddles and pools. Fungi, not seen in the bush around Kalamunda, were now common. Kookaburras yodelled, robins flitted across the path and black cockatoos called from afar and flapped noisily overhead.

Several Bibbulmun stage markers, fixed to posts, had been prised up; Waugal track signs were shot through; and water tank lids, secured with rivets, had been levered open and bent. Some people, it seems, cannot pass a sign or a marker without vandalising it.

Perhaps those responsible considered their vandalism an act of self-expression. Vandals, after all, actualise the human potential to be destructive. Destruction lies at the heart of modern ideas of self-expression, which demands the relinquishing of all connections to and responsibility for the world. Indeed, Abraham Maslow, the guru of the human potential movement and hence a founder also of the huge therapeutic enterprise subsequently built on it, defined the key component of self-realisation, or 'actualisation', as 'independence from the environment'. The individual, Maslow suggested, should strive to reject the external claims of the world, become his or her own master, and master of his or her own context. This is nothing but fanatical and dangerous nonsense.

Far from becoming independent, modern humans have become more and more dependent: on machines, doctors, therapists, economists, experts. This is not surprising. Mass consumption depends, like modern mass production, on discouraging individuals from relying on their own resources and judgments and on encouraging them to become consumers. Consumer society promotes the primacy of personal desire. We consume the earth because advertisers convince us that buying their goods will enable us to express ourselves.

Moreover, industrialism itself tends to discourage home production, enterprise and independent thinking and to make people dependent on the market, even for their opinions. In reaction to this pattern of dependence, disorientation and loss of control, people strike out against the world in frenzies of vandalistic 'self-expression'.

Carol and I reached the camp at stage 7A just at the start of another downpour. We took shelter in the toilet before beginning our now established camp routine. I string up a line for drying and airing bedding. We select a tent site, noting slope, obstacles, rocks and tie-off points for the tarp. We then roll out the tent, unfold the pole sections, thread them through the tent loops, snap them into grommets and position our low and intimate two-person tent under the tarp. Carol then takes off her boots to inspect the day's blisters. When the tent is dry and staked, Carol crawls in with sleeping pads and bags and arranges the bedding. We unpack the packs, take out a change of clothes and set aside food for dinner.

Other campers had lit many fires at this site. Although blackboys were common in the surrounding bush, most had the dry fronds of the underskirt broken away. Finding wood, especially dry wood, was also difficult, but we managed a moderate fire that burned through a couple of downpours and kept us up past dark.

The night was dry and cold, but the bush was still wet in the morning. A spider had spun its web between two trees outside the tent. Silken threads glistened with dew.

Our friend had warned us that the Bibbulmun was 'boring'. She found the Australian bush undramatic. For the most part, the land is marked by no deep gorges, no soaring mountains, no cascading cataracts, no massed congregations of wildlife and no spectacular, violent and bloody confrontations confirming the struggle for existence.

If we sat at our camp in the bush for a year, what would we see? Spring would turn to summer, summer back to winter. A kangaroo might hop by and graze, an emu wander through, a goanna bask in the sun. A tree or a limb, rotten with termites and age, might fall in a high wind. Birds would visit and insects hum; flowers would blossom, be pollinated, set seeds and germinate. But most of life in the forest, like most of life on the planet, is bacterial, beyond sight. Attending to these several orders of existence requires watchfulness and patience. The rewards are different from those that come from facing high excitement, speed, danger, record making and record breaking.

Even without overt drama, the bush pulses with life. Each day radiant energy from the sun pushes into the forest and strikes foliage, which absorbs carbon dioxide from the air and combines it with water sucked from the soil to make the sugars and enzymes that energise all life. These transformations release the oxygen that makes the air breathable. Oxygen-breathing animals consume plants and fertilise the soil. Soil organisms recycle plant and animal residue, releasing nutrients for the cycle of life to begin again.

Since rotting barely occurs in the dry jarrah forest, plants rely on periodic fires to incinerate the vegetation and deliver nutrients to the soil. Adaptations to fire include volatile oils in eucalyptus leaves that actually encourage fire, fire-resistant bark and seeds that drop after fire or contain food packages attractive to ants, which store the seeds underground out of the reach of flames.

Nevertheless, even in the jarrah forest, everything depends on the soil, a rich mixture of mineral particles, organic matter, gases and nutrients that, when infused with vital water, constitutes the fertile substrate for the initiation and maintenance of all life.

Just as all languages distinguish between things and events, so all cultures recognise the affinity, even the identity, between life and the soil. The second chapter of Genesis describes how God formed man out of the soil of the earth and blew into his nostrils the breath of life, and man became a living soul. In Hebrew, the first human was called *ha'adam*—a noun of feminine gender meaning of the earth, or soil. Only later was *ha'adam* differentiated into man (*ish*) and woman (*isha*) with the respective names Adam and Eve.

The indissoluble link between man and soil is manifest in the very name Adam. The word encapsulates human origins and destiny: our existence and livelihood derive from the soil, to which we are tethered throughout life and to which we are fated to return. Likewise, the name of Adam's mate, Hava (rendered Eve in translation), literally means 'living'. In the words of the Bible: 'And the man called his wife Eve because she was the mother of all living.' Together, therefore, Adam and Eve signify soil and life.

The ancient Hebrew association of man with soil is echoed in the Latin name for man, *homo*, derived from *humus*, the stuff of life in the soil. The Indo-European language root word for humus was *dhghem*, meaning 'earth'. This root also gave rise to the words *humble*, *human* and *humane*.

The universal distinction among language groups between things and events and the equally universal identification of soil and life prove that things and events, cause and effect, and soil and life do exist and are not socially constructed. In an important sense, there really is an affinity between the mind and the texture of reality. Common sense is accurate; there are things and kinds of things and actions out there in the world, and our mind finds them and labels them with words. This should not surprise. It makes evolutionary sense that creatures have an accurate understanding of the world. An organism capable of making successful predictions about future events will leave behind more progeny with those abilities.

Universal common sense characterised the Nyungar. Like traditional people elsewhere, the Nyungar lived a sensual life, a life close to the fecund earth. This was not only reflected in their word for themselves, *Bibbulmun*—a people and a land of many breasts—but also in their word *boujera*, which simultaneously meant birthplace, territory and the actual dirt or soil. *Boujera* thus merged soil and fecundity and recognised the irreducible fact that the source of life lay in the fertile earth.

Other cultures made links between the soil and life. According to the Tsimishian, Haida, Bella Bella, Tlingit and Kwaikiutl tribes of the North American Pacific Northwest, Raven created the earth, the moon, the sun, the stars and people. Raven first created humans out of rock. Rock, however, made humans too durable, so Raven used dust to make them mortal, as they remain today.[5]

The forest depends on the soil; the forest *is* the soil. Over millions of years, soil organisms changed the earth's surface from an aggregate of mineral particles to a mass teeming with life. Soil organisms make soil. They decompose plant litter and break down minerals into forms taken by plants as nutrients. They absorb moisture, aerate the soil and provide pathways for the transmission of water. Mycorrhizae fungi form tight symbiotic relationships with plant roots. They pass on nitrogen and phosphorus and enable survival for both. The exchange can easily be disrupted.

Industrial forestry and its consequences—erosion, compaction, fertiliser and pesticide use, toxin pollution, burning and exposure—alter soil ecosystems, decimate soil biota and compromise the soil's capacity to nurture life. A few centimetres of topsoil that may have taken hundreds of years to form can be lost or rendered biologically inert or even lethal in a single day of logging. The soil that brought life to the jarrah forest now also brings death.

Death was evident alongside the track that Carol and I walked when we left our camp at 7A. The bare limbs of dead jarrah trees reached to the sky above a bushy undergrowth encouraged by a recently defoliated canopy. Other jarrah trees, their leaves yellow, looked near death. Underneath them, dying banksia dropped brown leaves.

Dieback affects about 15 percent of the jarrah forest (or some 300 000 hectares) and is spreading at the rate of 20 000 hectares a year. In some blocks infection reaches 50 percent. These figures are conservative.

The true extent of infection is unknown and unknowable. Mass collapse often occurs after summer rainfall in certain areas. Infection cannot be predicted.

Dieback is caused by *Phytophthora cinnamomi*, a soil-borne fungus, most likely non-native. In periods of warm, wet weather, such as during summer storms, the fungus invades root hairs and fine roots and rots the major vertical roots of the jarrah, almost choking off the water. When the hot, dry weather returns and the trees need massive amounts of water quickly, they are unable to take it up. They die within weeks or even days.

The first patches of dieback-infected jarrah were observed in the Darling Range near Karragullen in 1922. The dying occurred in the same area as the first major jarrah logging operations. Coincidentally in 1922 a plant pathologist in Sumatra published the first description of a plant-killing fungus found in cinnamon, *Phytophthora cinnamomi*. *Phytophthora* means plant destroyer. The genus includes *P. infestans*, a major cause of the Irish potato famine. No one at the time suspected a link between dieback and *P. cinnamomi*. Over the next few years, however, further patches of unexplained deaths of jarrah and understorey species were discovered.

How *P. cinnamomi* arrived in Western Australia is unknown—possibly in the soil bounding the roots of imported fruit trees. It is known, however, that the fungus's spores are spread primarily by human activity. In the 1930s the timber industry changed from rail to road transport. As new roads were pushed through the bush, large amounts of *P. cinnamomi*-infected soil were to be moved about on the wheels and underbodies of vehicles. Jarrah dieback spread. After the war the Forests Department, the Main Roads Department and local roads boards conducted a massive road-building program in the forest. Road builders took gravel from areas with dead and dying vegetation and spread it over a wide area.

By the 1950s the forest had been plundered, not only by more than

100 years of logging but also by coal mines, tin mines, quarries, gravel pits, sand pits and rubbish dumps. Dams, pipelines, powerlines and the roads that linked all these activities further fragmented the forest. The result of all this plundering, the culmination of 100 years of management, was a depleted, impoverished and weakened forest that fell to the wasting disease caused by *P. cinnamomi*. Dieback became endemic.

In the 1960s researchers established a connection between jarrah dieback and *P. cinnamomi*, although not to every scientist's satisfaction. The Forests Department, in particular, was unable and unwilling to admit a link between logging and the dying of the forest. The department, after all, had built an empire based on the belief that nothing so final or so thoroughly beyond human control as the death of a forest could occur. Nature, the Forests Department believed, was endlessly malleable to human ends.

By the 1970s, however, the extent of dieback could no longer be denied. More than 200000 hectares of Crown land, ranging from shrub-heaths to tall forest, was infected, and the infection was spreading rapidly. In response, the Forests Department placed much of the jarrah forest under quarantine. Quarantine did not mean an end to logging, however. It meant only that vehicles entering or leaving the area on forest roads had to be cleansed of soil that might contain *P. cinnamomi*.[6]

By our seventh day on the trail almost all of the Bibbulmun track we had walked till then had passed through dieback-quarantine area. One species of bird seemed to be benefiting from the widespread dying. Black cockatoos feed on the grubs that live under the bark of dead trees, and we had noticed several flocks, both red tailed and yellow tailed.

On the ground we noticed the tracks of a party of walkers who had passed this way in the last day or so. They had broken small trees and branches, scratched the word FUCK in the sand, and left a trail of candy wrappers (which Carol picked up).

The track followed the Nifty Formation of the previous day. A brook trickled nearby. Although we hardly noticed gaining or losing elevation, the track passed into another watershed: the South Dandalup River. This river ends at Lake Banksiadale, behind South Dandalup Dam, which inundates 13 kilometres of river valley. Across the river the track started to gain elevation, slowly at first, then rather steeply for the last kilometre or so up the side of Mt Wells to campsite 8A.

We arrived in full sunshine and named the camp Drying Out. There was no pit toilet, but a water tank, bent and crumpled from vandal attacks, stood by the side of the gravel tourist road to the summit of Mt Wells. We spread our gear over the ground. Carol took off her boots and put her feet up to the afternoon sun, hoping to hasten the healing of her blistered toes.

As day faded to darkness, we kindled a fire in the lee of a large log. Stars appeared, and we felt the evening chill. We huddled together on the log until the fire burned low. We went to bed.

Morning dawned clear and cool. The track down Mt Wells passed through thick forest regrowth and was overgrown, covered in fallen leaves and slippery with jarrah nuts. We scrambled over or walked around the logs and fallen branches that lay across the path. On several stretches Waugal markers were infrequent, difficult to find or missing. At one point we missed a turn and walked several hundred metres the wrong way. We returned to the last sighted Waugal and resumed the path in a different direction.

This area, part of the Murray River watershed, the last undammed river in the jarrah forest, had been intensely logged and relogged. Signs of past logging were ubiquitous: old logging roads and railway beds criss-crossed the forest, and huge blackened logs lay on the floor where they had been left nearly 100 or more years ago. The area's main mill was at Pindalup, stage 9A on the Bibbulmun track and the next campsite after Mt Wells. Little remained of the former busy town: some stone and concrete foundations, a few pieces of corrugated iron and the outlines of streets marked by compacted, sterile earth where nothing grew.

Although the site contained a pit toilet and a water tank, we decided not to stay. We did not care to camp amid ruins. It was not quite noon, and the road to Dwellingup, our first resupply depot, was only about 6 kilometres away. We decided to walk to the road, hitch to Dwellingup and pick up our food package.

For nearly half the remaining walk the path paralleled a discontinued railway line, then turned left back into the bush. We then walked through a regrowth area of exotic gums, planted in straight lines, and reached the Pinjarra–Marradong Road.

We had barely unshouldered our packs when we heard a loud roar. A petrol tanker appeared over the crest of the hill. We put out our thumbs. Air brakes hissed. The tanker took 75 metres to stop, and we ran to catch up. We stowed our bags on the chassis of the prime mover and climbed into the cab with the driver.

With 40 000 litres of petrol behind us, we raced towards Dwellingup. On either side of the road lay paddocks of rich green grass spread before farm houses backed by tall forest. We were eight days and 140 kilometres from Kalamunda.

4

Till earth is as
barren as the moon

Dwellingup is a small town, consisting of one pub, general store, post office, cafe and a few houses. Carol and I found lodging in a self-contained holiday flat behind the cafe. The proprietors told us that we were not the only walkers on the Bibbulmun. An older woman called Charlotte, walking alone, had passed through a few weeks before.

On the track we had grown accustomed to a daily routine. We took our time and lived steadily and mindfully. Suddenly, in Dwellingup, we were overcome by haste and errands and chores. By dusk we were fatigued, an unusual feeling.

Next morning we spread our maps over the table and traced the route ahead. Ever since the morning we had left the scouts asleep in their tents at Abyssinia Rock, we had neither seen nor spoken to anyone else on the track. The next section seemed unlikely to prove so remote and unpopulated. It followed well-travelled roads, crossed farmland as well as forest, and passed dams, pipelines and tourist attractions.

During the rest of the day we dried our clothes, cleaned our gear and unpacked our box of food picked up from the post office. As our Bibbulmun guidebook recommended, we visited the local CALM office to inquire about conditions on the route ahead. The officer we spoke to was uninformed about and uninterested in the Bibbulmun. We called our friends in Fremantle, Peter and Suzie, and they confirmed that they would join us for a picnic on the Bibbulmun the next day.

The next morning we packed. Although we had replenished our food supplies, our packs were lighter than they had been at the beginning. We were sending heavy, superfluous items back to Perth: camera, bird and wildflower guidebooks, clothes. Peter and Suzie arrived at noon, after a trip from Fremantle that took them a little over an hour. They brought steaks, fruit, stove fuel and mail. Together we drove out to Nanga Mill, by the Murray River in Lane-Poole Conservation Park—stage 10E on the Bibbulmun and a few kilometres south of where Carol and I had hitched a lift with the driver of the petrol tanker.

Peter cooked the steaks on the steel plate over a fire in the grassed picnic area. While we were eating, a kookaburra flew onto the table and grabbed one of the steaks. I had to wrestle the meat out of the bird's beak.

Kookaburras are not native to Western Australia. Introduced in the late nineteenth century by acclimatisation societies in an effort to make the local bush sound more 'Australian', kookaburras have been disastrous for small endemic mammals and reptiles that are not adapted to their predatory presence.

After lunch we took a walk by the Murray along a section of the Bibbulmun. In this moist and favoured spot we passed some big jarrah trees; the undergrowth was tall and luxuriant. Suzie and Peter found it hard to believe that this was not old-growth forest. In an old-growth jarrah forest a tall, dense canopy, made up of well-spaced giant trees, reduces light penetration sufficiently to prevent the growth of dense understorey. The understorey in the Lane-Poole Conservation Park is dense. I pointed out further evidence of logging: massive stumps and big logs on the forest floor. Few really old jarrah survive, anywhere. Here and there a few trees had survived the first logging because they had hollow or twisted trunks. Since fellers expended great effort in cutting down a tree in the early days of logging, they took only the best.

Peter and Suzie were curious about how we lived while in the bush. We demonstrated the erection of our three-pole tent, assembled and lit our small stove, and explained how all our food could be cooked in the single pot we carried.

When Suzie and Peter had left, Carol and I were on our own again. We took a walk around the old town and mill site of Nanga. Kikuyu and other exotic plants overran the heavily compacted ground. Elsewhere, large pines shut out the light and carpeted the ground with dead needles.

As dusk descended, heavy clouds moved across the sky. A storm blew in and rain began shortly after dark. Thunder and lightning boomed and flashed throughout the night. Rain fell steadily. Inside the tent the air was hot and humid. We slept poorly.

In the morning we packed our soggy tent and damp bedding and made breakfast. We were soon ready to walk. The track followed the valley of the Murray River. The river, to our left, at times broad, at times narrow, flowed over rocks, collected in pools and flowed on. Morning birds called from vivid foliage.

Although undammed, the Murray River is not untouched. Much of the upper reaches of the catchment have been cleared for grazing and cropping. Water and salt run-off into the river have increased. The loss of fringing vegetation has opened the banks to erosion and the bed to increased sedimentation. Along those sections of the river that flow through Lane-Poole Conservation Park, blackberries are rampant. Although fresh water from numerous forest tributaries helps dilute the saline water from the inland agricultural areas, the river is still brackish when it reaches the Darling Scarp.

The track turned right, away from the Murray River, and followed Big Brook, a tributary. Soon we reached designated site 11A, a damp but pretty camping spot by the brook. Because we had not walked very far and there was plenty of daylight left, we decided to try for the next stage. The track, tending south again and still following Big Brook, climbed out of the Murray River valley. With greater elevation and drainage the bush became dryer. We crossed the divide and entered the watershed of the Harvey River. Soon we came across the emergent Harvey River itself, at this point hardly more than a trickle. Shallow puddles flooded the track and drained into rivulets that ran on either side. The air was damp.

Everywhere throughout the length and breadth of the jarrah forest, through all the undulating bush and across the various watersheds, the predominant colour of the soil is red, the hue of iron oxide. These soils, leached of silica and suffused with an accumulation of iron and aluminium oxides, are called laterites, from the Latin *later*, meaning brick. Such soils were commonly used to make bricks.

The laterite forms a hard layer of cap rock over underlying granite. The layer increases during long dry periods when the water brought to the surface from deep soils evaporates and leaves behind iron and aluminium solids. White sands and china clay remain at the lower levels. Subterranean soils containing high amounts of aluminium are known as bauxite.

The lateritic soils of the jarrah forest are nutrient poor, even by Australian standards. This has discouraged agriculture and favoured the perpetuation of a forest industry. Unfortunately, low soil fertility favours

P. cinnamomi. Impoverished soils do not encourage the microbial life that is antagonistic to the pathogen.

Unfortunately also for the jarrah forest, laterite can indicate the presence of bauxite. In the 1950s prospectors found that the biggest, healthiest jarrah trees grew in areas with the deepest bauxite deposits. This is because bauxite soils may be as deep as 30 metres over large reserves of water held in the white sands and china clays. Jarrah trees, adapted to long summer droughts, sink deep roots into this reserve. During the late 1950s and early 1960s, drilling teams systematically surveyed the entire forest, spread *P. cinnamomi*–infected soil throughout the forest, and located extensive bauxite deposits.

The Western Australian government, eager to accelerate forest exploitation, quickly prepared legislation authorising mining in state forests. Typically, government spokesmen denied that mining would damage or permanently change the forest. In 1961, when introducing a bill granting Western Aluminium (a precursor of Alcoa) a mining lease over 1.2 million hectares of the northern jarrah forest, Charles Court, the minister for industrial development, assured state Parliament that the area to be mined would not exceed 12 hectares a year:

> It is anticipated that the total clearing for the first year would be in the order of 30 acres [12 hectares]; and for subsequent years, and as long as the company was on an output of 550 000 tons per annum, 25 acres [10 hectares]. I stress these acreages because I think it has been conveyed in the public mind that huge areas will be involved all the time, and we will have ugly scars all over the place from one end of the State to the other.[1]

Court was wrong on all counts; everything that he assured Parliament would not happen, happened.

Mining began in 1963 with a mine near Jarrahdale. In the next sixteen years, the area of forest cleared increased 20-fold, from 12 to 250 hectares per year, and kept on increasing. By the early 1970s additional mines had opened at Del Park and Huntley. In 1984 clearing reached 300 hectares of bush per year for an output of 13 million tonnes of bauxite ore. By the following year there were five bauxite mines in the forest and four alumina refineries. Two companies besides Alcoa, Pacminex and Worsley, held bauxite mining leases. Mining companies now proceeded to double both extraction and forest clearing. By 1990 bauxite mining was destroying forest at the rate of 600 hectares per year. The total area of forest destroyed had passed 7000 hectares.

Miners entirely efface and burn the forest above bauxite deposits. The topsoil is bulldozed away and the cap rock drilled, blasted and excavated along with the underlying bauxite down to a depth of 4 or 5 metres, often deeper, sometimes down to the clay. No trace of the original jarrah forest remains after mining; nor will a true jarrah forest ever appear again. But destruction is not confined to the actual mine. Each site generates a widening circle of disruption, including haul roads, fire tracks, soil stockpiles, conveyor belts, machinery yards and buildings.

Abandoned mine sites were first planted with exotic pines, then with eucalypts not native to the jarrah forest, including spotted gum (*E. maculata*) and red mahogany (*E. resinifera*). The Forests Department chose the replacement tree species in the hope of restoring bauxite-mined areas for timber mining. Their priority was 'to grow a forest which has the potential for eventual sawlog production'.[2]

As Carol and I approached campsite 12A we saw two packs leaning against the marker post. Other hikers on the Bibbulmun? So far, except for the scouts at Abyssinia Rock, we had seen no bushwalkers. We took the side track leading into the campsite. An older couple appeared, but they were not walking the entire Bibbulmun, they told us. For several years now, they had been walking sections. On this trip they had come in on a side circuit from Collie and were heading for Dwellingup. They had decided not to stay at 12A but to move on. We could have the site to ourselves.

It was a fine camp. There was no rubbish and fresh water flowed nearby in the incipient Harvey River. We had walked a long distance and, because of fatigue after a restless night, Carol had begun to feel the strain.

That night we lit no fire but stayed up to watch the stars come out. Whatever else may have changed in the world, the cosmos remained the same. The stars we saw belonged to the same constellations that Georgiana Molloy had seen when she first gazed into Southern Hemisphere skies upon reaching Western Australia in 1830, and to the same constellations seen by countless generations of Aborigines. The unchanging (at least by human scales) heavens connect us to all those who have come before.

But there are disconnections even in the sky. The night sky is not quite as bright, and not quite as black, as it was for Georgiana Molloy. Urban civilisation has blurred the once strong contrast, the difference between light and dark, that our ancestors took for granted. There is now no black like the black the first settlers and the Aborigines felt and saw all around them. The restless surge of civilisation has deprived the world of pure dark. Everywhere there are almost as many lights attacking the black over the earth as there are stars in heaven. Even below the remotest horizon of the deepest bush and desert, there is a ceaseless vibration of light, not illuminating anything but depriving the world of the rest that the perfect black gave the Aborigines.

The busyness and unease that have deprived the world of pure dark have also robbed it of pure silence. The world no longer knows the difference between quiet and noise. There is now nowhere, not even in the interior of Australia, for great stillness to speak the profound language of silence. All over the earth the constant vibration of technology disturbs the air and generates an unease of sound and noise: aeroplanes roaring across the sky; bulk carriers and supertankers surging through the oceans; trains, trucks and cars clacking and grating across the vast distances of even uninhabited places; four-wheel drives droning and churning through the sand and dust of the Western Desert; and, in the jarrah forest itself, bauxite conveyors rolling and rumbling as they carry the earth out of the bush. All this noise stirs the silence that once enveloped the earth so that, even if sound is not heard, the precision of the silence is lost and its voice strangled.[3]

Most days and nights on the Bibbulmun Carol and I were deprived of even the semblance of silence. When we crossed Brookton Highway, we entered Alcoa's prime bauxite reserve area. Even when out of earshot of traffic or the drone of aircraft, we could hear the clamour of a distant mine. But the extinction of silence is only one of the consequences of mining.

Bauxite mining utterly confounds soil profiles—forever. It also permanently disrupts drainage, eliminates native forest and replaces it with an impoverished wood farm of even-aged eucalypts with thick understoreys, which is markedly different from true jarrah forest, with its highly distinctive, diverse and longer-lived understorey.

The nature and scale of mining, involving intense activity, massive earth movement, numerous machines and vehicles, and wide dispersal over area and season, spreads disease and causes the maximum possible destruction of the jarrah forest. The resulting patchwork of pits and unmined areas further fragments and degrades the forest.

Apologists for mining, such as Charles Court, in the beginning denied permanent change; they later embraced it. Foresters, who had always been dissatisfied with the jarrah forest as it was, began to see mining as an opportunity to create an entirely new landscape. They aimed to remake the land. In the early 1980s CALM (the Forests Department's successor) described mining, in combination with other management schemes, as 'a whole landscape treatment projected to be carried out over much of the non-saline forest zone in the next three to five decades'.

Other commentators were more honest. Barry Carbon, a former CSIRO scientist and head of the federal Environment Protection Agency, stated, when environmental manager for Alcoa, that 'the bauxite mining industry will be catalytic in removing the Jarrah forest from the Darling Range, and it will be unnecessary to manage the area as a Jarrah forest.'[4]

The dispassionate acceptance of, even enthusiasm for, forest destruction by foresters and scientists stems from their common underlying belief that the first duty of the human race is to control the earth. Carbon understood that bauxite mining had irrevocably changed the forest. Foresters assume, without any evidence whatsoever, that the changes will be for the better. This is wishful thinking. It too reflects an underlying belief—a matter of social convention rather than a product of logical methods and procedures—that it is the duty of foresters, scientists and managers to progressively artificialise the earth for the benefit of individuals, corporations and nations.

The ability to willingly destroy the jarrah forest takes a special kind of hatred for nature and a special kind of arrogance that, although distinctive, is increasingly common in the modern world.

At campsite 12A morning dawned fine and cool. Carol and I rose early, breakfasted and packed. We left the marked Bibbulmun trail and took a track that followed Harvey River. We liked walking by flowing water. Our route rejoined the Bibbulmun at Hoffman.

Millars built a steam-driven mill at Hoffman in the late 1890s. From the mill, railway lines radiated into the surrounding forest. Tree-fellers lived in camps at forest sidings. Horse teams dragged the logs to the railway. As an area was cut out, the entire camp—wives and children, huts, tents, household chattels—was loaded on railway trucks and taken to the next logging area. In this way the whole forest was cut over and the logs drawn to the saws.

The first mill at Hoffman burned down in 1917. Millars built a replacement on the banks of the Harvey River in 1921 and another mill nearby in 1924. Both mills operated until 1930, when the first replacement mill burned down. The remaining mill continued operation until 1961, when devastating bushfires swept through the central jarrah forest and destroyed the mills at Dwellingup, Nanga Brook and several other places. Surviving mills, including Hoffmans, were closed and the buildings dismantled. Millars built a new central mill at Yarloop. Mechanisation ended the need to locate mills in the forest near logging areas.

At Hoffman Carol and I ate a morning snack under a grove of even-aged, evenly spaced, exotic eucalypts, planted on the former mill grounds. Nearby masonry and concrete foundations had supported the mill's boilers. Raised and compacted embankments once carried railway lines. Wooden bridges, now sagging and rotting, spanned the Harvey River.

Everywhere in the forest, the past builds the present. The past will be there tomorrow and long into the future. There is no escape from the past. Its traces are deeply etched into the land and engraved in the characters of those who inhabit the present. Only fools promise a future free of the past. Only fools believe that in the future we will somehow escape the ugliness and degradation we have inherited and created.

Unfortunately, we live in foolish times, times obsessed with the future. In the future, proclaim the progressive prophets, humans will at last realise their true potential. For humans are wonderful beings, able to manage, able to solve everything, able even to steer the planet in its orbit about the sun. Futurists thus affirm and ensure the perpetuation of the very beliefs about control and conquest that underlie past and present human destructiveness.

The future is especially popular with politicians and scientists. They are attracted to the future because it is indefinite, beyond scrutiny and beyond accountability. Their future, however, is not exactly the name for what can reasonably be expected to happen, such as knowing that the sun will rise tomorrow. Rather, it functions as a blank, an open field for fantasy, a realm for wishful thinking. The word *future* is now used as the name for a simple, endless technological heaven. The pros-pect of a dazzling future distracts believers (in technology, in management) from the present, therefore excusing immediate crimes and confusions.

Politicians and scientists welcome the future because they believe it must be better, because it is the logical next step, and because the present pace of life almost makes it seem as though the future were already here. But equating the hectic pace of modern life, which includes a great deal of triviality, waste and duplicated effort, with forward movement is a mistake.

We cannot escape the past. The past reaches through us into the future. But the vision of a future free of the past and free of the present suits the modern mind, wherein both identity and the physical world have lost their solidity, their definiteness and their continuity. Indifference and antagonism towards the past and the present and towards the organic earth, so inextricably rooted in the past and present, characterise modern politics.

In response to the observation that industrialisation has led, continues to lead and will lead to extinction, degradation, congestion, squalor, pollution and corruption, leaders reply that we face a challenge. The challenge, politicians tell us, is to accommodate ourselves to endless growth without sacrificing quality. The real challenge is to convince people that they can have it both ways. We can enjoy our cake and at the same time destroy it. We can transform nature into boom times, jobs for thousands and extraordinary wealth for the powerful minority of land speculators, timber merchants and developers who stand to profit from what they call growth.

This argument hardly requires an answer. The much vaunted challenge is a lie. All industrial development involves a trade-off: in order to make room for more growth, the physical world has to be sacrificed. Growth does not happen in abstract space, but on the ground, in forests, in rivers and streams. All growth consumes and wastes the earth's material substance: air, land, trees, soil, water.[5]

5

Written in water

Despite human efforts to overcomplicate civilisation and oversimplify nature, life goes on. Some restoration takes place, even on the most brutally treated land.

When Carol and I finished our morning snack at Hoffman, we followed the Bibbulmun along the insurgent Harvey River. Writer and naturalist Loren Eiseley once commented, 'If there is magic on this planet, it lies in flowing water.' The air along the Harvey River was moist and full of the smells of decay and growth. The vegetation, now given a chance after 70 years of continuous logging, was vibrant and lush. As we walked, the river itself grew stronger and stronger, ever enlarged from the many tributary streams draining this luxuriant and wet watershed. We were enchanted.

We reached campsite 13A, a clearing by the river. But the day was early and the walking enjoyable, and we did not want to break our stride. The Waugals led along Harvey River Road, and so we kept to the track—at least we thought we did. Seventy years of exploitation had left a vast overlay grid of roads. One could hardly walk 100 metres without coming to a junction. Somewhere along the way we took a wrong turn and the Waugals disappeared. We kept to the general southwest direction that we knew the Bibbulmun to be heading. After about 4 kilometres we came upon a newly graded road we could not correlate with our maps. We were lost.

Down the road I heard a grader, a noise that had been reverberating through the bush for the past hour or so. I left my pack with Carol and hurried off in search of the sound. Fifteen minutes later, I hailed the operator. A CALM truck drove up. The driver and his offsider, a university student on work-study, after having spoken to Carol down the road, offered us a lift back to the Bibbulmun. They were in the forest, they said, checking routes for an upcoming Rally Australia race. They dropped us at Five Mile Bridge, a junction on the Bibbulmun.

We were tired. We had broken stride and had hardly eaten. After a short rest at Five Mile Bridge, we followed the Waugals along Dingo Road, which climbs and twists through the bush and parallels Harvey River on its final run into the reservoir behind Stirling Dam. We did not intend to go far and kept a lookout for likely campsites. In less than a couple of kilometres we came to a steep sidetrack that descended to the river.

A small clearing fronted the river bank. Upriver, the water flowed rapidly between granite banks, tumbled and slipped over rounded boulders and swirled into two pools before rushing on. We pitched the tent beside the lower pool. On the opposite bank the bush had been eliminated. A *Pinus radiata* plantation grew in its place. Behind us, the muted grey and green native bush spread up the hillside. We stripped and stepped into the rocky shallows of the upper pool. The water was cold, fierce, exhilarating. That night we fell asleep to the sound of water making its way over granite.

Next morning we followed Dingo Road as it looped round the indented shoreline of Stirling Dam reservoir. Almost all the area had been cleared of bush and planted with pines. Several rally drivers, checking the roads in preparation for next week's competition, roared past us. We had hoped to follow the track across the dam wall, but the reservoir was over-flowing, and a metre of water spilled over the top. We took an alternative route, a steep descent that passed in front of the dam. At the bottom we splashed across the outflow. This water ends up behind Harvey Weir. Most of the impounded water behind Stirling Dam and Harvey Weir is used for irrigation.

From the foot of the Darling Scarp, the Harvey River, in its natural state, meandered in a northwesterly direction across the coastal plain through wet flats and swamps to drain into the southern end of the Harvey Estuary, then, via Peel Inlet, to the sea at Mandurah. This pattern has been entirely disrupted. Most of the Harvey River's tributary streams, including Logue, Bancell, Yalup, Samson and Drakes Brooks, have been dammed. The wetlands have been drained, the river straightened and deepened and a drain, dug during the 1930s, diverts most of the river's water directly to the sea. The water that does reach Harvey Estuary is polluted with nutrients that cause massive blooms of blue-green algae.

Below Stirling Dam and across the Harvey River, Carol and I began to ascend. The climb was so steep and overgrown that we had to scramble up through the brush on our hands and knees. Heartbeats resounded in our heads. We reached a plateau, paused, then walked on to designated campsite 14A. The site was dry; there was no water tank and no nearby stream. We kept walking and soon began a steep descent into the water-shed of the Collie River.

The Collie River marks a rough division between the northern, drier jarrah forest and the southern, wetter jarrah forest. Although the trees look the same, associated species reflect the difference. Understorey plants common in the south occur only in wetter valleys of the northern part of the forest. Shrubs such as water bush (*Bossiaea aquifolia*) and the native willow (*Oxylobium linearifolium*), common in the southern forests, are rare in the north. The only native Western Australian member of the Podocarpaceae family, the koolah (*Podocarpus drouyniana*), occurs in the southern jarrah forest as well as in the neighbouring karri forest. None of these differences confers protection against dieback.

Although jarrah is the only eucalyptus susceptible to *P. cinnamomi*, the disease attacks many species of the jarrah understorey, particularly those from the Proteaceae, Epacridaceae, Dilleniaceae, Xanthorrhoeaceae and Papilionaceae families. Once infection starts, the susceptible understorey dies first. The common blackboy (*X. preissii*) and zamia (*Macrozamia riedlei*) often appear yellow and chlorotic. Bull banksia (*Banksia grandis*), in particular, dies rapidly once infected and is considered a 'good indicator' of the disease's presence.

Bull banksia is the only banksia that grows on laterite in the forest. Other banksias prefer sandy or riverbed soils. Both jarrah and bull banksia grow taproots up to 40 metres long into the moist clay layers. Roots of jarrah and bull banksia may occur together, and their common root channels are reused by successive generations of trees.

In mature jarrah forest bull banksia was relatively rare. The ground was open, and most shrubs were less than 1 metre tall. The forest canopy ranged from 20 to 25 metres, with some dominant trees 6 metres or more above the level of the mature co-dominant trees. Fires running through the relatively light litter and ground cover rarely damaged the crowns.

Logging and management completely changed the species mix and the fire cycle opened up the forest and encouraged the growth and spread of bull banksia. In the past most fires burned during the summer drought.

Summer fires are hot and most plants have seeds that germinate only after hot fires, especially the nitrogen-fixing acacias and legumes. When the Forests Department decided to manage the forest with 'prescribed burns', however, the fire season changed to the cool spring. Instead of encouraging the soil-fertilising legumes, spring fires favour marri trees and bull banksia.

Prescribed burns also spread *P. cinnamomi* to the highly susceptible bull banksia, which then pass the disease on to jarrah, where the entwined surface roots collect in the wet laterite cap rock.

The impact of dieback varies. In drier areas jarrah is relatively resistant to the disease, but it cannot cope in the wetter soils found in valleys and slopes, where the fungus invades all its surface roots. Sometimes trees die suddenly; sometimes gradual deterioration of crowns occurs. New leaves often sprout following the death of the main leaf-bearing branches, but the epicormic shoots are reduced in size. The cycle can repeat itself over many years, but each regeneration is less than before, until the tree eventually dies. Islands of survivors may exist in varying degrees of health. Dead trees may occur next to living trees. Some trees may take 10–20 years to succumb.

The result is the same. The dead jarrah and dead understorey mark an irreversible decline in the diversity of vegetation in the infected areas. Marri and other resistant species colonise old dieback sites, but the replacement growth is floristically impoverished compared with what was there. The variety of animals associated with the forest also declines. The consequence is a progressive decline in the life of the forest.

But the dying is not confined to the jarrah forest. *P. cinnamomi* infects at least 1000 hosts, half of them Australian. The floristically rich banksia woodlands and heathlands along the south coast, from Augusta to Albany, are highly vulnerable and suffer from some of the greatest impacts anywhere. In some places, 90 percent of the plants are dead. Whole species and whole vegetation types may be exterminated. The rare and susceptible feather-leaved banksia (*B. brownii*) is threatened with extinction; all of its few known locations are infected. Diverse woodlands of the bird's nest banksia (*B. baxteri*), scarlet banksia (*B. coccinea*) and the showy banksia (*B. speciosa*) are replaced with impoverished sedgelands following infection. Many wildflowers are also affected. Their death causes the disappearance of nectar-feeding animals.[1]

The moist watershed of the Collie River encourages farming, and much of the country Carol and I crossed after descending from Stirling Dam was cleared. The Bibbulmun followed the fence lines of cattle and dairy farms. The track was straight and geometric; where it turned, it turned at exactly 90 degrees.

The couple we had met two days before recommended that we camp along Zephyr Road, by the Brunswick River. There were some 'wonderful sites' there, they said. But we were not induced to camp: Zephyr Road was damp; enclosing thick forest shut out the light and made river access impossible. However, the day was late, Carol's knee was bothering her, we had walked more than 25 kilometres and she insisted we stop. At the end of Zephyr Road we found a side road down to a clearing by the river. Tyre tracks rent the ground. A couple of discarded tyres lay by the stream. Patches of oil stained the sand. Soggy toilet paper hung off the surrounding scrub. And here we stayed.

The stars came out before we went to bed, but rain started later in the night and fell throughout the morning pack-up.

From Zephyr Road the Bibbulmun connected several bush roads, including Mornington Road, which leads to Collie and Harvey and also provides access to nearby Worsley Alumina Refinery. For several kilometres the track followed the boundary of Worsley Timber Company. We ascended and descended a series of undulations. Each trough contained a flowing brook. At Worsley Siding we crossed a railway line, re-entered forest and emerged into farm country. The sky turned dark, rain loomed, then fell as we crossed the main Bunbury–Collie Road at the intersection with Wellington Dam Road. The Bibbulmun deviated back into the bush. Waugals became infrequent and the track indistinct as we pushed our way through flooded scrub. The track dried out and then descended through a blackbutt forest with a tall understorey and followed the rapid Gervasse River, which flows into the reservoir behind Wellington Dam.

Carol cared for no repeat of yesterday's marathon walk. We halted near a power line and a large, elevated water pipe. A side road led down to the river. In the light underbrush we cleared a space of twigs and rocks and sited the tent. We heard a dog growl and then bark. A pit bull terrier, wearing a collar, stood near the pipeline. What was it doing out here? Where was its owner? We thought it might be an abandoned hunting dog. It appeared timid, and it whined as it curled under the pipe to escape the frequent rain.

When the rain eased long enough to allow us to cook, the dog came over to visit. It was friendly but hungry. Carol worried about what was to become of it out here in the bush. I thought it might resort to sheep killing because there was a sheep paddock a couple of hundred metres away. At dusk two men in a pick-up truck left the paddock and drove in our direction. I stood by the side of the road and attempted to flag them down to tell them about the dog. They drove by without stopping. Their indifference surprised me. I wondered how many bushwalkers do they see in the bush who attempt to speak to them.

Rain came and fell steadily through the night. A few light showers at dawn did not interfere with breakfast or packing. After several days of rain, however, all our gear felt damp. Throughout the morning the dog remained curled under the pipe.

Today we looked forward to a less strenuous hike to a campground called Honeymoon Pool, below Wellington Dam. The track followed a fence enclosing a cow paddock. Cows grazed in company with an emu that followed us along the fence. Kangaroos bounded out of the way. The track joined a pipe and power line right of way where the bush had been cleared for a width of 50 metres. A sealed road led us the last several hundred metres to Wellington Dam and its picnic areas and parking lots.

Because the tourist season had not yet begun, the place was deserted. Carol tried calling the local ranger to report the dog, but the phone did not work. The kiosk was closed. Under its sheltering veranda we set up the stove and cooked felafel and pancakes. A group of observant, opportunistic magpies flew down. They ate banana chips out of our hands. A pair of shy corellas stayed in the background.

After we finished cooking, we walked to the dam-viewing platform. Eighty metres below us a massive concave wall of concrete rose from the bed of the Collie River. Behind the dam a great pond of water—solid, flat, motionless, still as death—reached into bays and indentations. Carol was appalled and fascinated. She wanted to know how a dam worked.

We followed the track below the face of the dam. Halfway down we met two workers, to whom Carol reported the abandoned dog. They told us they were about to monitor the dam wall, which was honeycombed with tunnels, and invited us to see the inside. We left our packs by the track and followed our guides across the face of the dam to a steel door near the centre.

Once inside, the workers set up their instruments to measure cracks in the wall. The data were used for estimating dam movement. They gave us directions and sent us on our way. We climbed up and down ladders to several different levels and walked from one end of the dam to the other. Water seeped through everywhere. Salt crystals formed over cracks, hung like stalactites from the ceiling, covered the walls in sheets and corroded iron fittings. The water behind the dam was so salty, the workers explained, that it was unpotable and unfit even for irrigation. The outlet valve was opened every spring to scour about 30 million cubic metres of brackish water from the bottom of the dam, in order to lower the salinity of the stored water.

There was no mystery about the cause of the water poisoning. Much of the watershed behind Wellington Dam has been cleared. With the erradication of deep-rooted native plants, particularly jarrah, the watertable rose. As the water rose, it brought salt to the surface, streams became saline and swept the salt into the dam.

Meanwhile, a new dam had been built on the Harris River, a forested tributary of the Collie River, to provide fresh water to the district. The water authority hoped that surplus fresh water from the Harris River Dam could be used to dilute the salt water behind Wellington Dam.

Foresters, dam builders and water supply agencies view water as a commodity with two basic traits: quantity and quality. No view could be more limited. Water in the forest is like blood in animals. Water charges and shapes all life, flowing in the veins and arteries of all organisms.

Underground, when carried through soil, water sustains the life of plants, invertebrates and microorganisms, dissolves minerals, carries nutrients and waste products to and from organisms, maintains chemical equilibria and regulates temperatures. Above ground, water quenches the thirst of land animals, provides habitat for fishes, crustaceans and amphibians, transports sediments and dilutes wastes. At the edges of streams and ponds, water nourishes a flourishing vegetation.

As soil is the material substrate of life, so water is its essence. In a real sense, water is life. 'And with water we have made all living things,' states the Koran. The Hebrew word for rain is *geshem*, connoting substantiation. To the ancients, who could not perceive that rain is recycled water from the earth, water represented the substantiation, or material manifestation, of God's grace from heaven. The Hebrew word for heaven, *shamayim*, can be separated into *sham-mayim*, which suggests source of water.

The movement of water is continuous and repetitive—precipitating out of the air, falling, ponding, soaking through the soil, flowing, taken up by plants, transpired, evaporated and returned to the atmosphere—without beginning or end.

This cycle has been disrupted throughout the length and breadth of the forest and not only directly by dam building, logging, mining, road building and clearing. Infection by *P. cinnamomi*, which kills deep-rooted plants and reduces vegetation diversity, also disrupts the water cycle. In an uninfected, healthy forest 60–90 percent of the rainfall (depending on whether the area is one of low or high rainfall) is transpired. In an infected, dying forest the amount of water transpired is less. Water run-off increases, watertables rise, salt seeps to the surface and streams become saline.

Outside Wellington Dam Carol and I walked by the great column of water that thundered from the base of the wall, spouted 30 metres and crashed and dissolved into the Collie River. The Bibbulmun followed the river along the right bank. The track was narrow, rocky and undulating but vivid with vegetation and wildflowers. We had planned to stop at The Ferns picnic area, select a table by the river, spread our food before us and enjoy a leisurely lunch. We arrived in the middle of a cloud burst, sheltered under our ponchos and ate pumpernickel smeared with chicken spread. In another kilometre we reached Honeymoon Pool.

Because the campground was accessible by car, it was organised for the convenience of cars. Sites were designated and numbered. Firewood was provided, and there were several toilet blocks with flush toilets. We found an unintended benefit to these conveniences. The buildings had generous overhangs, and since rain looked certain, we selected a site near a shelter so we could store our gear and cook under the overhang if necessary.

A group of teenagers and adults occupied a nearby site. We exchanged greetings. I spoke with one of the adults and told him we were walking the Bibbulmun. He and the teenagers were from Maddington High School. Much of the school was participating in a relay effort to walk the entire Bibbulmun from south to north. Each group spent three days on the track. Maddington businesses had sponsored the trek by providing transport, camping gear and a mobile telephone. Carol talked to a couple in a campervan, who passed on a wet weather forecast for the coming weekend.

A shower fell while we were preparing dinner. We carried the stove and the food to the shelter. At dusk we walked through the mostly deserted campground and visited the group from Maddington High School. Carol asked if they would phone in a report of the pit bull huddling under the water pipe at our previous night's camp.

We were greeted by the group as the 'intrepid' hikers, admired for undertaking the whole track. We gathered around the camp fire and exchanged opinions on hiking gear, backpacking food and blisters. One of the teachers had started his teaching career in 1969 at Armadale High School, my last year there. I remembered him: shy, nervous and very young. He taught trigonometry.

Rain fell throughout the night, sometimes heavily. At dawn we shook the water from the tarp and packed. The school group proved surprisingly disciplined and got underway at the same time we did. They headed north; we headed south. A shower fell as we crossed the Collie River. To the west the river flowed for several more kilometres through a steep and forested valley before being impounded again behind Burekup Weir. Below Burekup Weir the remnant river flows across the coastal plain and picks up more pollutants. Its banks have been deforested and eroded; sediment fills its pools. When Wellington Dam is scoured each spring, high, sustained flows of brackish water inundate river fauna and flora.

After crossing Collie River, Carol and I began a long and steep climb. We paused to catch our breath and to admire the view of the bush in the Collie River valley. We passed a television and radio transmitter tower, and the track began a slight descent. For several kilometres it followed a sealed road. We resented walking on bitumen, lost our concentration and missed the Waugal indicating a turn-off into the bush. We walked another kilometre before realising our mistake, retracing our steps and rejoining the Bibbulmun.

The track now led through a mixture of bush and farmland. We walked down a fence line and lost the track again. We checked our bearings against the map and found a bush road that led back to the Bibbulmun. We passed by pine plantations and dairy country. The descending track was rutted and eroded.

At the bottom we reached Ferguson Road, with farms, houses and stage 18A, a little patch of bush surrounded by pine plantation. The prospect of camping there did not appeal. The yard of a church on the opposite side of the road seemed preferable: mown grounds, a water tank, toilets.

A man on a tractor who was cutting the grass by the roadside said no one would mind if we camped next to the church. But we wanted to hike and camp in bush country. Because the next section of the track promised little bush and much farmland, we decided to hitch into Donnybrook. Besides, it was Friday and if we did not get to town today, we would miss the chance to pick up our second box of supplies from the Kirup post office before Monday.

The first car along the road stopped. We squeezed our packs into the boot beside two bags of golf clubs. The driver and his wife were down from Perth for the day to look at rural property for their retirement. They took us, via a brief farm inspection, to Donnybrook. It was mid-afternoon.

6

Wealth
without life

Ever since Charles Lane-Poole and the advent of scientific management, the Western Australian Forests Department and its successor, CALM, have been run by people trained to manage the state's forests for wood production (silviculture). Training teaches foresters that their overriding purpose is not so much to protect forests but rather to develop resources. A consciously disseminated 'can-do' technocratic optimism imbues the organisations with a sense of mission and excitement.

To the industrial forester, trees are timber. The word emphasises the functional nature of a tree as a source of wood fibre. Language has always been an indicator of values and ideology, and the language of industrial forestry both reflects and shapes perceptions and assumptions. Silviculturalists call tree species that are not commercially valuable 'weed' trees, to be rooted out like dandelions from a domestic garden. Oddly shaped trees are 'culls', unusable for timber and again weeded out. Ancient trees with low annual growth rates are 'overmature' or 'decadent'.

Foresters call dieback-affected forests 'graveyards', a derogatory term that permits further degradation of the infected land through the 'salvage' logging necessary to 'harvest' wood fibre that would otherwise be 'waste'. Emotionally potent, the vocabulary legitimises violence and destruction.

Above all, foresters are committed to 'sustained yield'. A slippery concept, sustained yield emphasises commercial resource development. Inevitably, it came to mean maximum yield. But a maximum sustained yield is an impossible dream, a figment of the industrial imagination. Sustained yield generates not sustainability but progressive destruction.

Sustained yield destroyed the world's richest fishery, the Grand Banks of Newfoundland. When scientists began to manage Newfoundland cod fishing in the 1950s on the basis of 'sustained yield', they promised to assign 'safe quotas' to fishing fleets. They failed. The cod catch fell from 810 000 tonnes in 1968 to 150 000 tonnes by 1977. Scientists set new limits calculated to allow stocks to recover, promised a future of abundance and predicted catches of 400 000 tonnes by 1990. They failed again.

For a while fishing had never been better. During the 1980s, aided by subsidies, fishermen bought more powerful boats and new, accurate fish-finding sonars. Large catches suggested there were twice as many fish as scientific research suggested. But this was a delusion. The fishermen caught more fish than the sampling scientists because they went to warmer places where they knew cod congregated. The scientists' research vessel, on its random course, encountered empty ocean. This was the true picture. Under sustained yield, fishermen had been taking not 16 percent of the fish each year as planned, but at least 60 percent. But the scientists, bound by an ethos that emphasised perpetual yields of products, compromised and in 1990 set a new quota of 235 000 tonnes.

Suddenly, in 1992, scientists and fishermen realised there was not a single school of cod in the Grand Banks and certainly no cod old enough to spawn. The fishery had collapsed. Consumers, however, can still buy cod in Newfoundland supermarkets. The fish come from Russia, where new fisheries have been opened to sustained yield.[1]

Similar delusions apply in forestry. What foresters attempt to manage for sustained yield are management systems—simplified models of nature. They represent the foresters' view of how the forest works. The models bear no correspondence to the actual forest and are always biased towards production.

In 1972 the Western Australian Forests Department introduced the idea of multiple use, which was officially accepted as government policy in 1976 and further refined in 1977. Like sustained yield, the idea of multiple use was based on an industrial model: forest management that optimised profitable use while providing habitat for native plants and animals. Again, like sustained yield, multiple use proved a highly flexible concept, depending on the audience and the situation. However, it always meant maximum human benefit and maximum use.

More a defence against the criticism of conservationists than a clear management policy, multiple use, when put in practice, meant multiple abuse; it meant commodity extraction first and foremost. Forest, watershed and wildlife preservation had legitimacy only insofar as they occurred incidentally to commercial production in the managed forest.[2]

Much of nature, including the jarrah forest, is messy and multifarious, full of irregularities not reducible to abstract categories. Indeed, a Forests Department committee concluded that 'jarrah forest ecology . . . is very difficult to present concisely and is too complex as a guide to management'. But managers, by the very logic of management, must ignore and deny real-life complexity. Managers must have categories.[3]

Foresters' enthusiasm for multiple use reflects the modern lack of interest in diversity. Previous generations had a deep and abiding interest in diversity. And they did not equate diversity with categories. The love of diversity was the love of the specific, of the unique and of that which resisted categorisation. Foresters intent on manipulation and control find the study of specificity too slow and tedious. A forestry industry dedicated to profit and growth finds diversity too expensive.

'The aim of management,' according to the Forests Department, 'is the regulation of [forest] resources to best meet demand while protecting the forest from damaging agencies.' Not surprisingly, the department failed to recognise the most damaging agency of all: itself. Instead, managers reduced the forest's multiplicity to 'land use' categories or 'Management Priority Areas'. Each area was ascribed a primary (dominant) use and a secondary use. The principal criterion in determining use was 'economic viability': 'Are the proposed land uses economically gainful?' In the event of conflict between primary and secondary uses, the primary use (logging) would be favoured.[4]

In 1985 the departments of Forests and National Parks and Wildlife were amalgamated to form the Department of Conservation and Land Management (CALM). Despite the acronym, amalgamation did nothing to soothe critics of Western Australian forestry practice. Of the amalgamated departments, Forests was by far the biggest, and its values, emphasising wood production, prevailed. Those values sanctioned continuing destruction.

Destruction, by its very nature, diminishes every value except destruction itself and the values destruction requires: efficiency, production, growth, profit. Other values, which in other times might have been thought civilised—love, caring, respect, humility—are devalued because they hinder destruction.

Two years before the departmental amalgamation, the timber company Bunnings bought out Millars. Bunnings now became CALM's major client, with access to 80 percent of Western Australia's jarrah and karri forests and control of more than 84 percent of the hardwood market.

When Carol and I planned our Bibbulmun walk, we decided Kirup would be our second supply drop. Conveniently, the track passed through the town. But now, in the middle of the walk, nearby Donnybrook seemed to offer better prospects for resupply.

At the Donnybrook Information Centre we learned that Kirup post office was actually a room in the village tavern, open for two hours a day. Fortunately, on Fridays, it opened at 3.00 p.m. The Donnybrook information officer offered to drive us there on her way home when she closed the Information Centre at three o'clock. We reached Kirup in ten minutes and collected our food box from the post office as well as a parcel from my publisher: the cover proofs for my book *An All Consuming Passion*.

We then stepped to the side of the highway and put out our thumbs. A young man driving a dented and rusty 1966 Falcon sedan stopped. We opened the doors and slid onto broken and slashed seats. Empty beer cans rattled on the bare metal floor. The driver was nervous, smoked continuously and drove very fast. The steering was loose, and the car veered left and right. Between drags the driver told us that he was an itinerant worker, currently engaged at Bunnings timber mill in Pemberton. He was anxious that his employment not cause offence:

'I hope you're not greenies.'

'We are.'

'Oh well, it's just a job. I'm not married to the Bunnings' way of life.'

Anyway, he had finished his shift and did not want to think any more about Bunnings. He was driving to Perth for the weekend, determined to get drunk and have a good time.

At Donnybrook we crossed the bridge over the Preston River to Brook Lodge, a rambling U-shaped, timber-framed, asbestos-clad, dormitory-style building built for fruit-canning workers in the 1940s. We were the only guests. The proprietor, Terry, a young woman with young children, showed us a room with a wood fireplace and gave us change for the washing machine and a couple of free packets of washing powder.

I stoked the fire in our room and put up drying racks. The weather turned cold, windy and rainy. After we had unpacked and spread our gear and clothes to dry, we went out for fish and chips. It was a mistake; they tasted awful. We should have kept to trail food.

Next morning, Saturday, we rose to cold, blustery weather and attended to our gear. We cleaned and re-waterproofed our boots and gaiters, cleaned and seam-sealed the much deluged tent and repaired the tarp, which was unravelling along one seam. Later we shopped for groceries.

On Sunday there was frost on the ground. If we had been in the bush, we doubted we would have had enough clothes to stay warm. We repacked our food and rolled up our gear. We checked the cover proofs for my book and during the rest of the day wrote post cards and letters. We examined the route map and noted that on several sections of the next segment to Pemberton, the track shared the way with scenic drives.

On Monday we rose early. The day dawned clear and fine and warmer than the previous day. We walked to the grocery store but it was still closed. A shop assistant waited in the sun with us. She thought our hike 'marvellous'. We bought chocolate bars, then waited for the post office to open before walking to the end of town to hitch down South

Western Highway to Kirup, where we intended to rejoin the Bibbulmun.

Two builders, driving separate cars, pulled over. They both wanted our company, so we took separate lifts. They were partners, on their way to a job in Pemberton. Each, in his own car, offered to drive us the whole way. That, we explained (separately), would defeat the purpose of the walk—we were walking to walk, not to arrive. Neither driver had heard of the Bibbulmun, nor could they understand our motivation. Their only comment was that we had to be 'keen'.

At Kirup we visited the CALM office to inquire about the route ahead. No one had a clue. The staff knew little more than that the track passed behind the office.

Following its formation in 1985, CALM continued the Forests Department's war against the forest. In 1987 CALM released a new forest management plan. The proposals called for greater productivity from the forest, despite predicting that the level of logging would decline annually from 1992 onwards. The timber industry, which at the time meant Bunnings and Whittakers, did not believe logging would decline. Timber merchants knew they would never be excluded from the forest, which was, as it had always been, theirs for the taking. After the release of the 1987 plan, Bunnings and Whittakers invested in greater milling capacity and cultivated larger markets for jarrah and karri, both in Australia and overseas.

CALM was not alarmed by the timber industry's expansion. On the contrary, a bigger industry would enhance CALM's role and prestige and consolidate its wood production ethos. CALM and the timber industry were partners. They jointly opposed any proposals to restrict logging, including the extension of reserves, the retention of river and stream buffer zones and the limiting of logging in dieback areas.

In 1992 CALM abandoned its previous prediction that logging after

1992 would decline and proposed instead that the cut continue at then present levels until 2002. The organisation had reverted to form. Foresters had always rejected limits, and they were certainly not about to accept them now. CALM's foresters, ever responsive to industry demand, could always discover more wood.

Foresters see their task as one of overcoming limits, not establishing them. Accordingly, they regard biological considerations (such as dieback) as constraints on the economic yield. Each time limits appear, foresters re-evaluate the assumptions used to determine the allowable cut and raise the harvest ceiling. Assumptions most subject to revision included the number of years thought necessary to regenerate a mature forest after logging, the number of hectares the agency can successfully protect from fire, insects and disease, the amount of forest land considered suitable for timber production and the estimated amount of wood fibre volume in the timber base.

On the basis of a 'new jarrah inventory', foresters located approximately 37 000 000 cubic metres of jarrah not previously discovered. Accordingly, the harvest could be increased. Much of the additional timber was what had previously been left uncut or on the ground.

Under its 1992 proposals CALM also revised its dieback control measures. Previously, logging took place in the summer, when the ground was dry, in order to avoid spreading *P. cinnamomi*. Henceforth, CALM said, logging would take place year-round. CALM also proposed to reintroduce clearfelling—total destruction logging that involved stripping the forest back to bare earth—in jarrah forest, increase clearfelling in karri forest by 33 percent and increase marri logging by 64 percent. Unwanted vegetation was to be poisoned by herbicides.

CALM admitted that the new harvesting regime amounted to over-cutting, that is, logging trees at a rate faster than they regrow to the same size. But this should not cause concern, CALM assured its critics. Optimism can always overcome the shortcomings of silviculture. Forest productivity can always be revised upwards. Besides, past estimates had been unduly pessimistic. 'The resilience of the south west forests,' according to a government review that endorsed the 1992 CALM proposals, 'has been consistently under-estimated.'[5]

To further justify overcutting, CALM, well practised in the arts and language of concealment, introduced the concept of 'uneven flow sustained yield'. Accordingly, a cut that the endorsing review committee concluded was 50–80 percent above a possible conservative sustainable yield 'will not have a significant effect on the long-term sustainable yield'.

To disguise their true agendas, foresters have always resorted to euphemism and circumlocution. In Victoria, for example, foresters argued that mountain ash regenerated best in 'full sunlight'. Accordingly, clearcutting became the 'full sunlight method of regeneration'.

Almost all the euphemisms and rationalisations popular with Australian foresters have been plagiarised from the United States Forest Service (USFS). 'Multiple use', 'even-age management', 'sustained yield', 'uneven flow sustained yield', 'overmature', 'decadent', 'salvage logging', 'weed tree', even the 'full sunlight method of regeneration', were first used by the USFS. Australian foresters adopted the language, shamelessly and thoughtlessly, and applied it ruthlessly to the very different circumstances of Australian forests. What interested them was the power and usefulness of euphemism, not its accuracy.[6]

Environmentalists opposed CALM's harvesting proposals. But protestors took CALM's conservation mandate too seriously. Foresters understand that conservation derives from the verb *to conserve* and not from the verb *to preserve*. Conservation means a utilitarian maintenance of nature's ability to produce goods and services, rather than the preservation of nature as such. To CALM, conservation means 'wise use', with the emphasis on use. Thus, CALM views the forest primarily as an economic asset that should and must be developed. The agency functions not to preserve forest but to establish new industries, products and markets to justify intensive logging.

From CALM's Kirup office, Carol and I resumed our Bibbulmun walk. The track skirted pasture land covered in sheets of water from the weekend rains. Frisky and curious young beef.cattle followed us along the fence line. Kangaroos, disturbed from their resting places, bounded out of the way. The sky was clear and the day sunny. Wildflowers bloomed everywhere, open to the light. The track descended into the upper reaches of the Capel River watershed.

The Capel River flows west. Once out of the forest, below the Darling Scarp, it serves as a drain for coastal plain farms. Its banks have been denuded of fringing vegetation and eroded, sediment fills its pools, and nutrients and pesticides pollute its water. Near the sea, the river flows between levee banks.

No contouring had yet taken place in the forest, however. A short, steep ascent, which then dropped suddenly to a stream, was followed by another short, steep ascent and another stream. Waugals were frequent. In several places the Bibbulmun left the logging and fire roads and followed a path through the bush. Morning passed into afternoon. The kilometres slipped away. Soon we were on Creek Road heading for stage 21A. But the site was on a dry plateau, and our map disclosed no water there. Besides, it was near a communications tower and a sealed road and was surrounded by development. We decided we would rather camp in the bush. After about 16 kilometres, where the track crossed a small stream, we stopped.

A fire had run through the surrounding bush in the last year or so. The ground was black with charcoal, jumbled with fallen limbs and green with new growth. We pitched the tent in the middle of the road. In the late afternoon a dark cloud appeared over the western horizon. Expecting rain, we hung the tarp over the tent and secured it to the logs and small trees on either side of the road. After dinner the sky cleared. Twilight turned quickly to dark. It was too early to go to sleep, so we talked and strolled up and down the track under the evening stars.

A heavy dew overnight soaked the tarp but the tent remained dry. We rose at dawn. With spring advancing, the days were getting longer, and every morning the sun pushed dawn back a few minutes.

Eos, the dawn, is one of the most attractive goddesses in Greek mythology. At the close of every night, rosy-fingered, saffron-robed Eos rises from her couch in the east, mounts her chariot drawn by the horses Lampus and Phaëthon, and rides to Olympus, where she announces the approach of her brother Apollo, god of light.

Aphrodite was once vexed to find Ares, for whom she nursed 'a perverse passion', in Eos's bed. She cursed Eos with a constant longing for young mortals. Thereafter, Eos began a series of seductions.

On this and every morning Eos seduced us. Dawn is one of the prettiest times in the bush: shafts of light profile the still forms of the forest trees, dew or raindrops sparkle on foliage, early birds call from the understorey and the canopy.

After an hour of walking we reached stage 21A, climbed a small, steep ridge, then began a long and very deep descent into the Blackwood River valley through Ferndale pine plantation.

With a catchment of nearly 28 000 square kilometres, the Blackwood is the largest river in the southwest. It is also one of the most befouled and saline rivers in Australia.

Overall, 85 percent of the Blackwood catchment has been cleared. In the upper catchment, the source of most of the salt, 95 percent of the land has been cleared. Upper catchment tributary streams, loaded with farm run-off, are little more than drains. Degradation is severe: fringing vegetation has disappeared, river and stream banks are collapsing, soils are acidifying, remnant vegetation is dying and soil erosion is widespread.

All this degradation, according to CALM's executive director, Dr Syd Shea, can be excused. It should always be remembered, he told a conference on the Blackwood River in 1990, that destruction in the catchment 'has produced a huge amount of wealth and still continues to produce a huge amount of wealth. We must balance that wealth against the destruction.'[7]

Shea did not explain how wealth was more important than wholesome rivers, clean air, sound soil or robust forests. He did not consider the matter. Wealth creation is all-consuming and takes precedence over anything and everything else.

Nevertheless, such unintended candour, even when, as in this case, it serves to justify past and continuing destruction, is unusual. But for Shea, wealth is the ultimate criterion, the final good. Therefore, any amount of destruction can be justified in the name of wealth.

CALM is not usually so forthcoming. Most senior CALM bureaucrats and scientists do not want to appear to be justifying destruction. They spend enormous effort denying destruction has or is taking place. Denial underlies wood management plans that claim that the forest is resilient and that, despite massive disturbance through logging, dieback and mining, 'most of the forest still behaves as a natural system.' This is a necessary delusion.[8]

In the few instances where CALM does, at least implicitly, acknowledge destruction, the admission is always accompanied by a promise that the future will be different. Such future talk offers salvation by technical fix. Futurists place their faith in miraculous machinery and miraculous management. In the utopian future envisioned by CALM, everyone will grow wealthy without cost, the forests will flourish, Western Australians will consume forever and there will be no destruction.

CALM and its defenders rebut sharp, penetrating and unswerving criticism by labelling it negative. They want hopeful, positive criticism. What they really want is conformity and silence—in other words, endorsement. When organisations and people in power engage in controversial activity, they commonly dismiss criticism as negative. What they are really trying to do is control the terms and content of the debate.

But criticism, no matter how negative it may appear, is the first step towards understanding the mentality that grips CALM and other forest agencies in Australia. Besides, criticism is a citizen's duty and the primary means of exercising his or her legitimacy. It should never be compromised or qualified by the labels *helpful*, *positive* or *hopeful*.

7

An illusion,
a shadow, a story

During our descent to the Blackwood River, Carol and I followed roads torn up by the weekend's Rally Australia. At the bottom we came to the river itself: broad, dark, silently flowing.

The water beckoned. For a moment we wished we could climb into a canoe, flow with the current and live on river time, the particulars of our existence determined by the warmth of the sun and the river's flow. The moment passed. In walking we followed a different rhythm, and that was sufficient for now.

We followed the river upstream to Nannup–Balingup Road and crossed Wrights Bridge to Wrights Bridge campground, stage 22A on the Bibbulmun. Our map indicated a campground similar to Honeymoon Pool, with water and toilets, but there was neither. The grounds had been partly bulldozed and were strewn with rubbish and overgrown with exotics. On the river bank, among a patch of rank kikuyu, there was a fire pit and three picnic tables. The place had a tawdry feel. The river water was foul. We filtered it and added lemon flavouring but the brackish taste persisted.

Nevertheless, we decided to stay. Our feet hurt from the unaccustomed steep descent of the morning, and the map indicated no water within reasonable walking distance. We pitched the tent on the grass under large gum trees by the river and then looked for drinking water.

There were several farmsteads along the road. We crossed the bridge and called in at the first. It looked like a weekender. No one was home. From a rainwater tank out back we filled our canteens with sweet water.

Back at camp Carol studied the track book and maps. She plotted the next few campsites and read about the several circuit routes off the main track. She rued all that we would miss by not walking the side routes: the different forests, streams and small towns.

During the afternoon several parties of would-be campers drove through the campground and out again, disappointed, no doubt, to find a lack of those amenities widely advertised on CALM's maps. As we were cooking dinner, two young men in a pick-up truck drove in. They got out of their vehicle and walked down to the river. From Perth, they had taken a couple of days off work and were camping in the south. They reckoned we were 'pretty keen' to walk the whole Bibbulmun. Disappointed with Wrights Bridge, they said they would leave us in peace and return to a site they had visited 10 kilometres upriver.

Towards dusk I lit a fire. Night came. We sat at the table and stared into the flames and into the darkness beyond. We discussed my idea about turning the walk into a chronicle: 'the Bibbulmun book', we called it. But I had reservations. Literary convention demands narrative, demands change. Readers expect stories to grow towards the light, to tell some tale of direction, purpose and transformation. But direction and purpose I did not see: we were in the bush simply to be in the bush.

Western culture, at least since the eighteenth century, has proclaimed change as natural, constant and inevitable. The ideas of growth, progress and improvement that have dominated our view of the world for the past two centuries receive support from science and economics. The human potential movement and all forms of psychotherapy, with their focus on personal change, development and growth, also reinforce the modern prejudice in favour of change and against stability. And not just any change but purposeful, directional change, change always towards betterment and improvement.

This bias informs most modern stories, whether told by scientists, economists, psychologists or novelists. Therefore, how could I write a narrative, with beginning, middle and end, a journey story, without also reinforcing the modern bias towards change and progress, without reinforcing the very beliefs that underlie industrial civilisation's war on nature?

Yet, we live in a storied world. We try to make sense of our lives by telling stories about ourselves. Similarly, we try to make sense of other lives and of the world itself by telling stories. Narratives must tell a story—even in the absence of the modern prejudice towards progressive change—a tale that captures our interest as a series of unique events with interesting causal connections.

All cultures, at all times, have told stories. Stories arise out of the common human experience of living embedded in the passage of time. This commonality, our experience of the world, is a matrix open to all possible standards of judgment.

In nature, humans experience immanent things that do not appear to change and things, permanent and periodic, that do change—for example, the cosmic recurrences of days and seasons and natural disasters. But, perhaps most important for the purposes of storytelling, there appears an apparent direction to life, from birth and growth to decrepitude, death and decay.

Historians tell stories because they wish to make sense of the world. Like other storytellers, they see the past as a chronicle, a continuous register of events that actually happened and of people who actually lived, in a time that preceded our own. This chronicle is difficult, probably impossible, to understand without a plot, without a story. In fact, without a narrative there is no connecting thread—nothing to inform us how we are related to what has come before. Without stories we remain mute before the world.

But the stories we tell, and the structure and meaning they give the world, do not reflect nature. There is no necessary and dependent correspondence between our three-act dramas and the real world—nature is not so obliging. Rather, stories reflect a human perspective. Narrative, because it is universal, probably corresponds to something fundamental in human consciousness, not in nature. Stories about the world are always our stories.

What is the unvarnished story of the jarrah forest? Natural jarrah forest does not change so much as continuously recreate itself. It has been stable as a forest for thousands of years. Once it extended much farther than at present; once it may have covered less area than at present. But it was always a jarrah forest, unstoried, beyond human intention and reach. And this will not be explained.

How then could I make sense of what we had seen, contrive unifying themes and achievements from a plethora of diverse and scattered observations, without also imposing that story of purpose on nature? I had no answer. We went to bed.

The night was cool, and we slept soundly. A chorus of kookaburras heralded the dawn. Mist hung in the valley and rose from the river.

Sunlight broke through the haze and lit up the trees on the opposite bank. Cattle came down to the water's edge to drink.

We started walking in full and warming sunlight: a lovely day. Carol observed that, apart from the pine plantations and other development, the walk of the last few days had been through some of the prettiest wild-flower country so far. The bush was resplendent with scarlet runner (*Kennedia coccinea*), one of a large variety of plants belonging to the pea family that grow in the jarrah forest. They come in an array of colours— red being one of the most frequent—often with a touch of orange and yellow. Another group of pea plants mix yellows and browns, including the many flowers called bacon and eggs. Pea flowers also come in mauves or purples, often in early flowering varieties such as the hoveas. We saw the deep purple hovea growing everywhere. A fresh morning breeze filled the air with the faintly sweet smell of hakea.

For a while the track followed the Nannup–Balingup Road, beside the Blackwood River, on the opposite bank from where we had walked the day before. We turned off at the Department of Sport and Recreation camp of Lewana. The place was vacant. A couple of dozen cottages with barbecues, playgrounds and swings stood in lines amid rolling, mown and very green lawn under tall trees. A sign forbade cars on the grass, which was for 'the people'. How old-fashioned. When was the last time a government agency claimed to be doing or protecting anything for the people? Granted, 'the people' was always an abstraction, but modern rationales, like 'growth' and 'the future', are no improvement.

We tried a cottage door; it was unlocked. Inside, we found a fully equipped kitchen, a living room with a wood stove and bedrooms with bunks. Everything was tidy, almost regimented. Photographs above the kitchen counter showed how plates, pots and pans and utensils were to be stored. And, indeed, saucepans, frying pans, salt and pepper shakers, milk jug and knives and forks were stacked and sorted exactly as illustrated. Everything worked, including the hot water. We took showers and then sat in the sun on the porch of the main office and ate chocolate.

From Lewana the track followed Spruce Road, up a steep 2-kilometre embankment out of the Blackwood River valley. Here the bush had been extinguished and replaced by pine plantation. The air was still and the sun shone on our backs. Sweat soon soaked our shirts.

Although much of the Bibbulmun passes through dieback-quarantine areas, CALM routed the track so that walkers avoid the most infected areas, as well as areas recently logged. But places of devastation were not difficult to find. At the top of the embankment, Spruce Road forked. The marked Bibbulmun track followed the right fork. Our map, however, showed that if we took the left fork, Ellis Creek Road, we would rejoin the Bibbulmun in about 6 kilometres.

We soon reached a gate and a sign declaring Ellis Creek Road officially closed. We climbed over and kept walking. To the right and left the jarrah was dead and gone. The forest canopy and understorey had been completely effaced. In its place, smothering the dead tree trunks, a vigorous, bushy growth of marri had sprung up.

Marri (E. calophylla), commonly known as red gum, is the most widely distributed eucalypt in the southwest, where it occurs usually in mixture with jarrah or karri, rarely in pure stands. It regenerates readily, rapidly and prolifically from seed, coppice and lignotuber and resists drought, fire and dieback. Marri flowers profusely and is a major source of nectar for the honey industry. In the early 1970s the Forests Department dubbed marri a 'weed tree' in order to justify its use as a principal resource for the Manjimup woodchip industry.

Eventually the young marri in dieback areas will grow into some poor version of a forest—homogeneous and limited in use, the wood suited mainly for pulp. This will be, as far as CALM is concerned, the ideal forest. It will no longer be necessary to even pretend to manage it as a jarrah forest.

CALM originally established quarantine areas with the ostensible and sensible purpose of keeping out the activity and machines that spread the disease. But there was another agenda. Foresters wanted the disease to express itself, reveal its presence and thus allow the agency to map the extent of dieback infection and plan for future logging. Indeed, CALM's 1992 logging plans called for multiple incursions into infected and uninfected areas of the forest.

Under this agenda dieback was not so much a loss as an opportunity. Dieback gave CALM another excuse to redesign the forest, to concentrate less on managing natural forests and to focus more on converting them into timber plantations. Proposed dieback countermeasures—including fire, poisoning bull banksia, drainage, genetic engineering and fertiliser to stimulate antagonistic microbes—all aim to create a forest perfectly suited to human ends, a forest that is regulated, uniform, based on products, rigid, confined and short term.

This is what CALM means by management. Management produces and reproduces destruction. Practically every major management practice adopted by CALM and its Forests Department predecessor has spread disease, impoverished the soil, polluted the water, decreased diversity and fragmented, diminished and undermined the forest. Most management practices have failed, even on their own terms. Sustained yield has been nothing but a dream. Governments and forest agencies, not just in Western Australia but all over Australia, admit to overcutting. Sustained yield means extinction of the forest estate. It means a forest cut two or three times. Multiple use means multiple abuse. It means gold mines at Boddington, coal mines at Collie, tin and tantalite mines at Greenbushes, mineral sands mines at Capel and Waroona, more sand mines approved or proposed, bauxite mines at Dwellingup, Jarrahdale, Willowdale and Mt Saddleback and quarries for gravel, limestone, sand, rock and clay everywhere. Road building opened the forest to clearcutting and disease. Prescribed burning spread dieback and favoured the growth of susceptible bull banksia. All these events in the life of the forest were perfectly acceptable management practices in their day. And all were disasters.

These disasters are no accidental by-product of management. They are intrinsic to it. They are inevitable outcomes of the attempt to control and conquer nature. Yet, although management has been catastrophic, calamity only prompts calls for more management.

Managers justify management with science. Ever since the days of Charles Lane-Poole, management in Western Australian forests, indeed in all Australian forests, has been guided by science.

Science bequeaths philosophical as well as material legacies. Its great philosophical legacy is objectivity, or the scientific point of view. This means doubting everything except facts. It means adhering to the facts and letting the chips fall where they may. Among the 'facts' long accepted by science in Australia is the 'fact' that the country needs more people, and people need more saw logs and woodchips, more inventions and hence more science. The good life depends on the indefinite extension of this chain of logic. And the good life—wealth—as far as Dr Syd Shea, CALM's executive director, recognises, depends on destruction.[1]

No doubt many CALM scientists find Dr Shea's formulation crass. Like most scientists they believe their findings are objective, and they take the business of science to be simple—the establishment of 'objective' facts that look the same to everybody. Attitudes, they believe, must be and are irrelevant to this endeavour.

Science, however, is not a fixed body of established knowledge or truth but a developing body of ideas—ideas about how to think about the world. These ideas are not independent of that world. They are not in that sense objective. All intellectual inquiry, including science, draws ideas, presuppositions and metaphors from outside its borders. No form of intellectual inquiry can be self-sustaining. Conceptual borrowings can deeply affect its inner workings and invariably undercut claims to objective knowledge.

All scientific laws and truths are probationary. To be sure, truth that has been subject to rigorous investigation and survived is not to be taken lightly and is much better than a random invention that has not been put to the test. Science, in this sense, is far from trivial. But neither is science omniscient. It deals only in ideas of a particular kind and always lives with uncertainties. The ideas that form scientists' thoughts, the questions they ask, even the answers they give, are invariably influenced by social context.

The certainties of science are as pluralistic, as conflicting and as subject to opinion as politics or economics or any other human enterprise. The procedures of 'objective' inquiry are just as much modified by self, by fantasy and by folly as those of subjective inquiry.

One of the most pervasive fantasies in science is the bias of progress. Biologists, especially, favour narratives that unfold a story of meaningful progress. The story of life, according to the conventional narrative, begins with the accretion of a few molecules into cells capable of division. Life then moves on to ever increasing complexity, which eventually leads to sex, and finally, and triumphantly, to human consciousness.[2]

Equally as influential as progress in dictating the kinds of stories scientists tell is the idea of control and conquest. Indeed, the conquest of nature lies at the heart of science. Some scientists are more explicit about conquest than others.

During his tenure as head of the Commonwealth Scientific and Industrial Research Organisation, Ian Clunies Ross, for example, articulated science's preoccupation with mastery over nature. All science, he believed, turned on conquest. 'Only now,' he claimed in 1957, 'can we see the consequences of our growing conquest of nature, and within a decade we shall see appreciable evidence of that conquest even in the more inhospitable and intractable spaces of northern Australia.'[3]

At the end of our walk through the dieback-devastated land, Carol and I returned to the Bibbulmun and to relatively healthy forest bordered by pine. We lunched, then resumed the walk along an old and overgrown railway embankment, Toowong Form. After an hour we reached the day's destination, stage 23A, a clearing next to a pond. The water spread out behind a dam across a small creek. A very large, old jarrah log bordered the pond's edge. A great tangle of growth around the perimeter of the pond prevented other access. Carol suggested we call the place Ant Camp because of the enormous number of ants making their way over the log. Strong gusts of wind blew through the clearing, across the pond and into the bush beyond. Clouds scudded across the sky.

'Is that rain?' Carol wondered as she stood on the log and watched the surface of the pond erupt in dozens of small, ever widening ripples. It was, but, although the freshening wind and clouds heralded an incoming front, the deluge held off.

Dinner was insufficient. We had lived on the same food for three weeks, and it was no longer enough. We were beginning to feel hungry. To take our minds off food we lit a camp fire that, fuelled with wet pine cones, produced more smoke than flame. The air grew damp. As we stoked and poked the coals, large, heavy drops of rain started to fall. We sheltered in the tent.

Rain continued throughout the night. The last shower fell just before dawn. The pond was still again. We shouldered our packs and returned to the Bibbulmun, along Stallard Road. After a couple of kilometres, the road forked. The Bibbulmun followed the left fork. We decided to keep to Stallard Road and find our own way to Dalgarup Nature Reserve, where we expected to rejoin the track.

We were soon in dieback-infected country. The skeletal remains of dead jarrah punctuated the bush. The area had recently been logged under CALM's 'salvage logging' program. Log dumps lay by the road. In one clearing recently used logging equipment stood beside newly cut timber. Jarrah seedlings in plastic punnets lay by the side of the road.

For several days we had seen fresh emu manure but no emus. Manure was present again this morning. Then, up ahead, I saw the bobbing back of an emu disappear round a bend. We walked on. Suddenly, an emu with seven striped chicks at its feet came running down the track towards us. When it saw us, it panicked, veered left and right, unable to decide how to avoid us and shepherd the chicks at the same time. Carol and I stood very still. The chicks kept straight on down the track, more upset by their guardian's behaviour than by the sight of us. Ten metres ahead of us the adult took to the bush. The chicks kept coming. We thought they were about to run through our legs. One metre in front of us, six of the chicks turned into the bush. One squatted at our feet. I leaned forward, dropped my hat over it and scooped it up so we could admire its stripes. When I put the chick down, it joined its siblings by the side of the road. Carol worried whether they would find their guardian again, but I assured her that nature had not left parental bonds to chance. The binding of parents and offspring was one of the most conspicuous facts of nature. The male emu and his young would soon reunite.

Once we were through the logged area, the understorey thickened. Large hakea and grevillea grew above our heads. Blue lechenaultia (*Lechenaultia biloba*), which the Nyungar called piece of the sky, spread over the forest floor. We inspected the smaller flowers: common donkey orchid, spider orchid and, on a patch of gravel, a colony of black-eyed sundew (*Drosera platystigma*) with tiny, newly blossomed orange and black flowers. Above us, red-tailed cockatoos screeched and wheeled in the air.

We turned up Guy Road and rejoined the Bibbulmun in Dalgarup Nature Reserve. The track dipped and trailed beside a small stream. The bush changed. Suddenly jarrah gave way to karri. We entered Karri Gully, the first and northernmost grove of karri on the Bibbulmun. The air was cool and sweet, and the ground was littered with bark and leaves. A light shower fell as we started a 300-metre loop trail. We marvelled at the smooth white trunks of the karri trees that upheld a canopy higher than any we had seen so far.

8

Changes as the forest is changed

Karri (*Eucalyptus diversicolor*) is big. With crowns reaching 90 metres or more from a base 7–10 metres in circumference, mature karri trees are among the world's tallest trees. They grow only in the wettest areas of Western Australia's southwest, on deep, well-drained sandy loams over gneissic or granitic rock.

Karri grows straight with clear, smooth bark and few branches below canopy level, which, in a mature forest, forms at 70–80 metres above the ground. The species name, *diversicolor*, refers to the colour difference between the topside and underside surfaces of the leaf: deep green on the topside, paler green underneath. The canopy foliage is relatively open, plenty of sunlight reaches the forest floor and a dense growth of shrubs, creepers and small trees forms at ground level.

While jarrah can grow from lignotuber, karri regenerates only from seed. In an old-growth karri forest dense undergrowth inhibits the growth of karri seedlings. Germination depends on end-of-summer fires to clear the ground vegetation and consume fallen logs and dead branches. Karri seed, held in capsules high in the tree, ripens rapidly after a fire and falls onto the ashbed. Seeds germinate after rain and grow quickly in the fire-enriched soil. After two years seedlings may reach 3–4 metres in height. After twenty years a vigorous karri may reach up to 25 metres.

Karri grows in a more confined area than jarrah. Its range covers about 610 000 hectares, in a block some 160 kilometres long in a south-easterly direction from Nannup to Point Irwin and up to 50 kilometres in a northeasterly direction inland from the coast. An isolated stand of karri occurs in the Porongorups, north of Albany. Actual karri forest within the main karri area is small. Even before European settlement there was prob-ably only 216 000 hectares of karri forest in total.

Befitting the 'conspiracy of optimism' that has undone Western Australia's forests, the amount of karri has been greatly exaggerated in the past. In his enthusiasm for exploitation, John Ednie-Brown, Western Australia's first conservator of forests, greatly overestimated the amount of timber in the colony. He stated that usable timber covered 8 million hectares, of which 3.2 million hectares was jarrah and 485 000 hectares karri. This was more than twice the actual amount. The 1903–1904 royal commission on forestry estimated that karri forest covered 400 000 hectares. As recently as 1974 the Forests Department assessed the area at more than 300 000 hectares. No one concerned with exploitation ever had an incentive to underestimate or even correctly estimate the karri forest area.[1]

Of the original 216 000 hectares of karri, about 35 000 hectares has been cleared, mostly for agriculture. Of the remaining 181 000 hectares (just 0.07 percent of Western Australia's total area), more than half (98 000 hectares) has been logged. Most of the karri forest (163 000 hectares) is on Crown land under the management of CALM.

In the past logging in karri forest was less extensive than in jarrah forest. The trees were bigger, harder to extract and fewer uses could be found for the timber. That changed in the 1960s.

Until the 1960s there had been little international trade in wood-chips (used to make paper) because there were few ships prepared to carry a cargo with such a low weight-to-volume ratio. But in the mid-1960s Japan began building specialised woodchip carriers. Combined with a ferocious Japanese appetite for paper and packaging, the new carriers opened the planet's forests to an unprecedented level of plunder.

No forest was too remote for Japanese avidity, and no government was resistant to Japanese blandishments. Australian governments agreed to supply huge volumes of woodchips—produced by chipping trees clear-felled out of native forests. States competed against one another to sell their forests, at whatever price. Here was a chance to convert Australia's despised unproductive forests into productive ones. Woodchipping promised maximum wood production. A.C. Harris, conservator of forests in Western Australia, said of woodchipping in 1968: 'Through the medium of this industry we can see ourselves realizing the dream of all foresters—complete utilization.'[2]

Karri Gully had not yet been completely utilised. Carol and I walked through a forest where the air was still and heavy, suffused with the smell of dampness and decay. From high overhead came a gentle roar, like distant breakers, as a breeze stirred the high foliage. The canopy seethed with birdlife. Lorikeets dashed between flower-laden boughs. From ground level great volumes of exuberant green matter reached towards the light. Layers of dripping foliage hung off peppermints (*Agonis flexuosa*) and karri oak (*Casuarina decussata*). Under them grew thickets of broad-leaved karri hazel (*Trymalium spathulatum*), bearing small, creamy white flowers, shrubs of karri wattle (*Acacia pentadenia*), bearing masses of pale yellow, fluffy globular flowers, and tree hovea (*Hovea elliptica*), spreading rich purple through the forest understorey. Irises, trigger plants, orchids and mosses covered the ground. We followed the loop trail past beard heath, cutleaf hibbertia (*Hibbertia cuneiformis*) and sodden bracken fronds. Under cover and out in the open, stick-nest ants had built nest heaps from casuarina leaves.

From Karri Gully, Waugals led us down Brockman Highway. Vehicles, going to and coming from Bridgetown, sped by on the wet road. After a couple of kilometres the Bibbulmun turned left into the bush along Stallard Road, wide and gravelled. We were in wet jarrah forest and had also reached the upper reaches of the Donnelly River catchment. A power line passed overhead. Near a culvert a 1.3-metre tiger snake slithered off the track. It was the first snake we had seen since we began the walk.

A few kilometres from Brockman Highway we reached Willow Springs, a former logging and loading site, and our destination for the day. We looked for a tent site. Prospects appeared poor. The ground was damp, had been heavily compacted, recently burned and elsewhere was overrun with exotic shrubs and trees. Piles of bulldozed dirt abutted patches of scrub. We were tired and hungry. The weather turned suddenly cold and a shower threatened. After a bite to eat we explored the area further. On higher, drier ground we found a campground with picnic tables and fire pits. Bulldozed several years before, the ground was still raw. Bushy jarrah limbs sprouted from stumps. We decided to stay.

A nearby sign pointed the way to a walking track through an arboretum. The loop walk passed groups of eucalypts, labelled with common and Latin names, from all over Australia. The Forests Department had planted the trees to find out which species grew best under Western Australian conditions and therefore which species might best replace the logged jarrah and karri. The arboretum reflected the Forests Department's relentless quest (since assumed by CALM) for the dream of full utilisation.

No forest use promised greater utilisation than woodchipping. Throughout Australia in the late 1960s governments and foresters were ecstatic: native forests were on their way out. Clearfelling—projected to take place in areas called coupes, of 400 hectares or more at a time— afforded an opportunity to efface and replace Australian forests with plantations, either of softwood or hardwood. Foresters aimed to supplant the natural with the artificial in order to increase efficiency and profit. They planned to woodchip 8 million hectares, out of a total Australian forest area of 42.5 million hectares, or nearly one-fifth of the forest.

In 1969 the Western Australian state government passed the Wood Chipping Industry Agreement Act. The Act committed the state to supplying the Western Australia Chip and Pulp Company Pty Ltd (WACAP, a wholly owned subsidiary of Bunnings) with marri, karri and jarrah logs sufficient to produce 500 000 tonnes of chips per year for fifteen years after the date of the first export of woodchips. The logs were to come from an area that covered more than one-quarter of state forest and timber reserves and all but a very small fraction of the karri forest. Foresters projected coupe sizes of 800 hectares. In 1973 a new government increased the state's annual commitment of chip logs to 670 000 tonnes. Meanwhile, the federal government, in the belief that more was never enough, granted WACAP a licence to export 750 000 tonnes of woodchips per annum.[3]

Australian exports of woodchips began in 1970 from the Harris-

Daishowa mill at Eden, New South Wales. From the beginning, Australia was the largest supplier of hardwood pulpwood to Japan. Tasmania began exports in 1972, followed by Western Australia in 1976. Australian exports soared. In 1980 the Australian government again increased WACAP's export quota, this time to 900 000 tonnes per annum. As exports doubled between 1975 and 1989, so did the area of forest destroyed.

By the mid-1970s Australian governments had approved the clearcutting of 2 million hectares of forest for woodchips. In Western Australia, in the seventeen years between 1976, when woodchipping began, and 1993, 32 000 hectares of old-growth karri forest was clear-felled and turned into impoverished, even-aged regrowth. The clearcut area amounted to one-quarter of all the karri in state forests.

Clearfelling proceeded without any knowledge of the effect on soil fertility, leaching of nutrients and erosion, or on the salinisation, siltation and possible eutrophication (increase in plant growth due to an increase in nutrients) of water courses, or the impact on floral and faunal diversity. The main arguments in favour of clearcutting were economic and operational. It was simply more convenient to clearfell. Moreover, foresters liked clearcuts. Clearcuts allowed them to remake the forest according to their own specifications.

Foresters have always disparaged old growth. In a mature forest, growth and decomposition are relatively balanced. There is as much death as new life, and little or nothing is added to the inventory of 'growing stock'. Industrial foresters view this as a wasteful, almost tragic and immoral, lack of productivity. Young, rapidly growing stands, on the other hand, generate large increments in annual growth. Since higher growth rates justify increases in cut, 'overmature' and 'decadent' ancient forests have to go.

In Western Australia, Forests Department scientists claimed (claims since elaborated by scientists employed by CALM) that clearfelling simulated the natural reproductive strategy of karri and was therefore unlikely to have adverse long-term consequences. According to this scenario, cataclysmic wildfires periodically sweep through the karri forest, killing mature trees and stimulating seed-fall onto the newly created ashbed. The seeds germinate in the nutrient-rich soil and grow without competition from mature trees to form new, even-aged stands. In the absence of such ferocious wildfires, stands are likely to become 'overmature', even 'degenerate'.

No evidence has ever been produced to support this contention. Nature knows no such categories as 'overmature' or 'degenerate'. These are silviculture terms, nothing more than labels of convenience. They have no correspondence in the real world.

In the real world of a natural karri forest, up to one-third of a tree's functional existence comes after it has ceased to live and grow. During a tree's death and decay it continues to serve as habitat for animals and as food, rooting medium and soil builder for the next generation of trees. Old and dead trees, the bane of foresters, may be the richest source of life in the forest.

Australian forests, including karri forests, depend on a constant cycling of nutrients between the trees and the soil. Cycling allows a large forest biomass (the weight of organically produced matter) to develop on inherently poor soils. Tree removal, however, terminates cycling. Disruption is especially catastrophic under clearfelling. Clearfelling removes the bulk of the forest biomass and the nutrients that would otherwise be returned to the soil, either by rotting or by fire. New growth following clearfelling must depend on reserves of soil nutrients that are likely to have been incinerated, eroded or otherwise dissipated.

During the afternoon at Willow Springs, a car with two older couples pulled into the campground. After a walk through the arboretum, they approached us. They found the sight of bush campers unusual. They were staying at the nearby holiday village of Donnelly River and were on their way to a fishing spot. They liked Donnelly River and recommended the village restaurant. We were interested; after weeks of camp food, a restaurant meal sounded inviting. The two women were curious about our Bibbulmun walk. Their husbands, however, had little time for chatting. Their curiosity about us was quickly satisfied, and they were impatient to leave. 'Got to fish,' they said.

When we walked into Willow Springs we could hear logging trucks down the road. After dark we heard frogs, which boomed and croaked all night. But logging trucks were the first sound of the morning, coming even before the dawn kookaburra chorus. I nudged Carol awake: 'Listen to the kookaburras.' She turned and listened and fell back asleep.

The morning was cold and getting colder. I lit a fire and we warmed our hands over the flames. Carol sipped her coffee. The day was crisp and clear, and soon a strong sun rose above the forest that enclosed the campground. We started walking.

The track descended slightly to a tributary stream of the Donnelly River. We crossed a bridge and turned onto a road that followed the stream. The surrounding hilltops, sheathed in laterite, were covered in jarrah. In the valley laterite gave way to loamy soil and jarrah gave way to karri. The tall trees dwarfed the occasional passing vehicle.

We crossed the stream again, kept to the streamside track and passed a coupe of 55 hectares that had been clearcut several years before. The coupe, defined by straight edges and square corners, was covered with an impenetrable leafy growth of 4-metre-high karri. A CALM sign designated the area: *Regenerated Forest*. This bogus claim called for a little ecotage: *Generated Plantation from Devastated Forest*.

A plantation is not a forest and can never become a forest. Forests are evolved by nature over eons. Trees alone do not make a forest. In a forest a multitude of plants and animals coexist, both competitively and co-operatively, an expression of the intrinsic mutuality of all life on Earth. And life in a forest—soil, bacteria, water, trees, wildflowers and animals—belongs to the biosphere, to the order of nature.

A plantation is not a forest. Foresters cannot recreate forests, they can only contrive plantations. Plantations are engineered, managed, predictable and profitable, and represent short-term bio-industrial, productive systems. Their biotically limited existences belong to the industrial order.

Just as a plantation is not a forest, so too there is no correspondence between clearfelling and natural phenomena. Clearfelling does not duplicate nature. Natural events—fires, windstorms, disease attacks, floods—do not dissect the forest with roads, tear up and compact the soil with tracked vehicles, entirely efface the forest biomass or crush the crumpled ground with log dumps and staging areas.

Clearfelling represents silviculture preference, not nature. The dream of full utilisation, of intensively managed wood-fibre farms, demands replacement of natural forest with homogeneous, even-aged stands of evenly spaced trees that provide the greatest growth of the desired wood product in the least amount of time. Even-aged stands also facilitate efficient harvesting of the second crop of trees.[4]

The faith of the industrial forester in silviculture's ability to sustain intensive extraction of commodities—wood fibre, water, bauxite—from the forest requires a studied and persistent optimism, buttressed by economics and the worship of wealth. Furthermore, enough science backs the faith in technological mastery over nature that foresters can assert an empirical foundation, and therefore unquestioned legitimacy, to their beliefs. But forest researchers ask only the kinds of questions that advance the conspiracy of optimism. Research that exposes flaws in the faith is dismissed or simply indicates the need for 'additional studies'.

Foresters generally do not care to consider any ideas or evidence that would lessen their blind assurance that all is going well, or, if not going well, cannot be remedied by more research. Forestry-sponsored research, carried out after clearfelling, inevitably finds that the clearfelling produced no irreversible change and that the forest has remained healthy (despite its actual non-existence). Should any evidence of failure emerge (such as the recognition that the forest no longer exists), it is explained by forestry optimists as having resulted from shortcomings in research strategies, in application or in funding.

Faith in technology, in progress and in economic growth generates the belief that solutions—the technological fix—will be found without the need to alter the status quo and certainly without the need to reduce consumption. Trained experts backed by enlightened government policies will be able to sustain high levels of production from the forests.

Some scientists treat their findings with caution. They are aware of the complexities of nature, the overwhelming incompleteness of their knowledge and the bewitching power of language. They are also sceptical of research that always seems to enhance the interest of the researcher's sponsor. Caution and critical awareness do not characterise CALM scientists, at least those whose reports are vetted by senior management. With unabashed confidence they assume a categorical understanding of the nature of Western Australia's forests. Their research invariably confirms that what is best for wood production is also best for the forest. Their data always show management to be in the right. No matter what humans do in the forest—mining bauxite, spreading disease, clearfelling—all will turn out for the best. CALM lives by the faith that no permanent damage can ever be done by management guided by science.[5]

For a while Carol and I kept to the road along the looping stream that led to Donnelly River. Owing to the great tangle of intervening growth, we could hear the water but not see it. At the junction with Donnelly River, we crossed a bridge and took a side track. We pushed our way through the overhanging undergrowth. Several kilometres later we reached the village of Donnelly River.

Donnelly River, formerly known as Wheatley, had once been the site of a large mill built by Bunnings in 1948. Several hundred millworkers and their families lived in the company town by the mill. Steam engines and locomotives hauled timber out of the surrounding forest to the saws. By 1978 there was no more timber left, and Donnelly River Mill, as it became known, closed down. Bunnings closed the town as well. Later, entrepreneurs, who hoped to turn the area into a holiday centre, bought the buildings.

Carol and I walked the streets past rows of mostly unoccupied weatherboard cottages. A plague of rabbits kept the grass closely cropped. We waved to a woman sitting on a cottage porch. She said we had been expected. The two couples we had met the day before at Willow Springs had alerted the village to our arrival.

At the Boarding House Bed and Breakfast (the former single men's quarters) we met Ray and Sue, Donnelly River's owners. They showed us to our room and offered us orange juice and tea. We wanted something more substantial, however. At the general store we each had a hamburger, a meat pie, a milkshake, an ice cream and a packet of biscuits. Afterwards we booked a table at the restaurant for dinner that evening.

In the afternoon we toured the town again, swung on the schoolyard swing, visited the dam that supplies the town's water and walked by Jack the Squatter's shack. Jack, an immigrant from eastern Europe, had worked at Donnelly River Mill for thirty years. When the mill closed, Ray and Sue told us, he refused to leave. He came with the town.

Ray and Sue also told us that Charlotte, the woman ahead of us on the Bibbulmun by a few weeks, had also stayed at Donnelly River. This was her second trip down the Bibbulmun. She travelled very light, ate only rice cakes and peanut butter, never cooked, never lit a fire and was in her tent by 5.30 p.m. every night.

We also heard some current news. On Wednesday, on the evening we had camped by the small pond and felt the fresh wind and the deluge after dark, a tornado had passed through Mandurah. On the other side of the continent, Sydney had won the right to host the Olympic Games in the year 2000.

We arrived early for dinner and met our host, Dena, in a small room in one of the village's many weatherboard buildings. We sat at a wooden table, covered by a tablecloth, lit by a candle and decorated with a vase of flowers. We were the only customers. Numbers vary, Dena said, but her husband, the chef, made no less an effort for two than for twenty-two. We started with an appetiser of smoked trout over salad with yabbies (small freshwater crustacean) and prawns, had sirloin steak and locally raised marron (freshwater crustacean) for the main course, and finished with pecan pie and fresh strawberries. We could have eaten more.

9

According to the
gospel of getting on

Wealth, according to CALM's executive director, Dr Syd Shea, justifies destruction. Shea's praise of wealth is not unusual. We live in a culture ruled by the market, and the market is based on the idea that there can be no such thing as enough. A better future means more of everything. Yet, in spite of having so much, we remain hungry. In our quest to satisfy the insatiable, we are devouring the earth.

This never satisfied quest has not been true of all humans at all times. It is a peculiarly modern undertaking, sanctioned by story. Modern stories exalting wealth began with Adam Smith, who, in 1776, published *An Inquiry into the Nature and Causes of the Wealth of Nations*. Insatiable desire, Smith believed, previously regarded as morally suspect, could make the world turn and generate material abundance, which, he added, must come before anything else.

In the *Wealth of Nations* Smith explained how, under the market economy, the actions of millions of buyers and sellers, each bent on nothing more than finding personal opportunities for exchange, give rise to a vast system of mutual coordination. Each individual, Smith wrote, 'is led by an invisible hand to promote an end which was no part of his intention'. In the market the pursuit of individual self-interest results in competition. Acquisitiveness, constrained by competition, continuously adapts production to the changing wants of the market. In the market the interaction of supply and demand guarantees a supply of goods at precisely the price individuals are prepared to pay for them.[1]

Smith's *Wealth of Nations* was much more than a treatise on economic principles. The book's real significance lay in the story it told. Smith outlined a history of the gradual economic progress of human society that suggested an indefinite future augmentation of wealth and wellbeing.

Subsequent glosses on Smith's major themes became more formalised and began to feature a character called Economic Man. Economic Man was an abstraction, a fictional creature with an abacus (later a pocket calculator) for a brain. Oriented always to the future and eschewing fellowship, Economic Man was entirely rational, devoid of emotion, utterly self-absorbed, single minded, systematic, calculating and constantly weighing gain against loss. He had no motive other than pure economic self-interest directed towards one thing: increasing his own wealth.

The concept of Economic Man arose in conjunction with the modern theory of rights, of identity and of individualism. These ideas have been intimately associated with the rise of capitalism and mechanistic science. All shared the same assumptions: nature was devoid of intrinsic meaning or worth, and society was nothing but a collection of egoistic individuals motivated by appetites and aversions.[2]

Flesh and blood men and women—men and women who loved, hated, sang, danced, bonded, betrayed, cared, forgot and begat—played no role in economic thought after Adam Smith. The subject became one dimensional. Economic exposition assumed a near-deathlike quality.[3]

When I studied economics at university, I was struck by the general flatness and blandness of the subject and of those who championed it. Economists, in their books, articles, lecturing habits and general conversation, were narrow, dull, fixated and characterised by a truncated range of emotional response. Economists knew nothing of what it is to be alive—open to joy and exaltation, to pain and suffering, and to folly and grace. Later, I saw a similarity between economics and autism.

In autism the affective basis of life is faulty, undercut by neurological damage. In normal people reason is founded on feeling. Understanding involves and requires feeling, not merely thinking. It is feeling that gives rise to affective relationships with other people and with the rest of the world.[4]

By contrast, as in autism, there is something mechanical about the minds of economists. They lack some of the 'subjectivity', the inwardness, most people have. Economists have a 'stickiness of attention', so that there is great tenacity on the one hand but a lack of agility and pliability on the other—apparent, for example, in the turgid prose style typical of most economic writings.

Feeling, emotion and desire in general may not be missing—economists are certainly capable of violent passions, intensely charged fixations and fascinations—but sympathetic feeling in relation to complex human experiences, particularly social ones and love of nature, is absent. Certainly, economics has been and is characterised by indifference, amounting to hostility, to the natural world.[5]

Economics takes the life out of the world. Economics turns concrete living nature—forests, water, trees, wildlife—into lifeless abstractions—resources, wealth, profit, utility, return on investment. Abstractions are manipulable by the methods of economics; nature is not. In the stories economists tell about the world, nature is written out of the narrative, and so are most humans. Instead, the one-dimensional, autistic character Economic Man stands at the centre of their chronicles. Nature is reduced to a sphere of pure externality, a stage set for the pursuit of economic self-interest by Economic Man.

All stories convey ideas. Ideas animate the human world. People live under the spell of ideas, good or bad, true or false. And ideas influence action and bear upon the living earth. The idea of Economic Man, and the idea of progress that accompanies him, have had devastating consequences for the land. The idea of increasing wealth and the perception of reality it encourages have been applied to the Australian landscape with a ferocity and ruthlessness unmatched anywhere in the world. Nowhere else on the planet have so few people pauperised such a large proportion of the world's surface in such a short period of time and for such transitory gain.

Despite the unaccustomedly rich food of the Donnelly River Restaurant, Carol and I slept well. We woke early in the soft bed in the small pink room of the Donnelly Bed and Breakfast and listened to the birds attracted to the village's forest margins.

In the bright sunlight of early morning we walked down to the mill. Rabbits scampered across dewy grass, uncut logs lay among skid lines and rusting machinery sprawled under open corrugated iron sheds. A kangaroo hopped along the inside of the mill fence, seeking a way out.

At the Boarding House Ray served breakfast: cereal, toast, bacon, eggs, a tomato slice and a potato cake. The morning sun promised a fine day, and soon we were on our way, following an unpaved road out of the village. In a few kilometres we rejoined the main Bibbulmun track.

The day's route, which tended in the direction of the Donnelly River, meandered widely, as did the river. The Donnelly River is one of the least disturbed rivers in the southwest. Some of its catchment has been cleared for agriculture, but much is intact. For most of its length the river flows through state forest. Because we wanted to see as much of the river as possible, we ignored the Waugals and followed Donnelly Drive, which kept closer to the river than the Bibbulmun.

We crossed several bridges as the river looped left and right. Tannin-coloured water flowed steadily over a gravelly bed between well-defined banks fringed with vegetation. The river flowed south, west, south, east, north and south again. We passed a grader and stopped to talk to the operator. He confirmed that people camp at the picnic grounds at One Tree Bridge, our likely destination. If we had any trouble, he said, we were welcome to camp on his land, opposite the picnic grounds.

The track turned east for several kilometres then abruptly changed direction south. We passed recently cleared land, private logging operations and farmland. The track left the road and wound through bush towards the river. We stepped over a fence and walked through low-lying swampy ground. On higher ground we came upon two lads camping. They were evasive, seemed to regard our presence as intrusive and replied in monosyllables to our questions about directions. They looked like they were up to no good. As we left we saw the metal Bibbulmun marker for stage 25C on the ground near their camp.

We followed Waugals across a paddock, slipped under a fence, crossed a log bridge and walked through the bush to Green Island campground, a flat, heavily trampled, rabbit-infested piece of land with several steel fire rings and enclosed on three sides by the looping Donnelly River. Mosquitoes swarmed. The site did not appeal.

Our map showed that the Bibbulmun continued another couple of kilometres along the river to One Tree Bridge. We decided to camp there. In the absence of a stage marker for 25C, we missed the turn-off to the riverside track. We followed farm roads to Donnelly Drive, which led to sealed Davidson Road. We had gone several kilometres out of our way and were still a kilometre from One Tree Bridge. But we did see something we would have otherwise missed. Davidson Road passed the Four Aces—four very large karri trees growing in a perfectly straight line. They had probably sprouted from a nurse log, the rotting trunk of a long-since-disappeared downed karri.

Along the road we saw the grader operator we had spoken to earlier in the day, now at his farm. We waved. By the time we reached One Tree Bridge, we had walked 25 kilometres. It was late afternoon, the sun was low in the west and the trees cast long shadows. We pitched the tent near the huge karri tree that once bridged the river and gave the site its name. Wide enough to allow the passage of a horse and cart, the original log sits on the river's bank and is a tourist attraction.

Early next morning, a Sunday, two fishermen walked by our camp on their way upriver. Soon after we left and made our way down river. We crossed the bridge at Davidson Road and turned onto a riverside track. We pushed through some fringing scrub and emerged into open karri forest.

Masses of purple hardenbergia festooned with clumps of white clematis and entwining orange-red kennedia trailed up the recently burned slope to the left. Below us, to the right, the beautiful Donnelly River flowed through a thick and green understorey of karri oak, karri wattle and bull banksia. The massive trunks of tall karri trees cast long shadows over the undergrowth and the river, crossed at several places by natural one-tree bridges.

Several side tracks led down to the river and to some splendid camping spots. We walked on. The map showed the track crossing and recrossing the river. But the old wooden bridges at these points were closed. Signs warned that they were unsafe. Normally, we ignored such warnings, but the first bridge we encountered was twisted, sagging, rotten and missing planks. We took the detour and scrambled through scrub and forest on the steep river bank. The river flowed south and west. The track turned east and entered forest cut into squares by logging roads.

Foresters cannot imagine anyone having legitimate objections to clearcuts. They characterise complaints about clearcutting as simply aesthetic objections. Under that reductionist assessment, they design clearcuts to be less visible to tourists and travellers by leaving strips of trees along major routes to cloak logging devastation from public view. CALM routed the Bibbulmun with a similar aim in mind.

We were not to be fooled, however, and shortly after leaving the Donnelly River we took a detour. At Palings Road, a wide, well-graded and banked logging route ripping through the heart of the forest, a large sign cautioned: *Prepare to Stop*. A subversive Green had added the word *Logging*.

Designed for trucks and heavy equipment, Palings Road leads straight to the Bunnings Diamond Chip Mill, outside Manjimup. We ignored the signs warning that Palings Road was closed to the public and set off for an uncensored view of forest destruction.

Owing to the opposition that woodchipping aroused, the Forests Department reduced its recommended maximum coupe size in the 1970s from 800 hectares to 200 hectares. But 200 hectares is still a very large clearing. In any case, actual size depends on economic considerations, and the maximum is sometimes exceeded when two or more adjacent coupes are left with little or no uncut forest between them.

Regardless of individual coupe size, the forest is still destroyed. Clearcuts along Palings Road attested to the realisation of CALM's grotesque dreams of full utilisation. The timber had been trucked out, and tractors and bulldozers had knocked over and ripped apart every remaining plant, treated the debris as rubbish and dragged and pushed it into heaps, ready for burning. Elsewhere, holocaust fires had left white ash, charred limbs and blackened stumps and had demolished soil architecture. Such fierce fires do not duplicate wildfires in an unlogged forest.

Contrary to foresters' protestations, the secondary forest here will not be the same—ever. It will be depleted of nutrients, limited and impoverished. But by then, most of today's foresters will be dead.

Foresters claim that clearcutting emulates nature and that modern management considers all aspects of the forest. But no one can know the full details of a forest community, which is made up of numerous organisms, many of them as yet unidentified, and whose behaviour and biological characteristics have not been defined. Foresters who make such claims of omniscience are either self-deluded or knowingly fraudulent.

Whichever they are, the scientists and technicians behind CALM's indefatigable schemes for destroying the forest represent the peak of modern forestry: trained in management, proficient in self-delusion, expert at disguising their destruction behind circumlocution. They are being sent to advise on the management of South American and Southeast Asian forests. Thus is linked the global assault on the forests.

Meanwhile, the ransacking of Australian forests continues. A November 1997 agreement between the federal and Tasmanian governments allows increased logging of Tasmanian native forests over the next twenty years. The federal government further agreed to lift all limits to woodchip and whole log exports and to provide legally binding assurances that prevent future governments from saving forests. This Regional Forest Agreement is likely to provide a model for other state governments that wish to plunder their forests and prevent citizen involvement in conservation.

Foresters dismiss critics as ignorant. Only 'people unfamiliar with natural processes', according to one senior CALM scientist, object to clear-felling. Exclusion is an excellent debating tactic; it ends debate. CALM's defenders divide the world into two: insiders and outsiders, the informed and the ignorant. The latter have no place in the debate.[6]

Another good debating tactic is to dismiss opponents as emotional. Foresters, in contrast, have reason on their side—as if a commitment to forestry, production, profit and remunerative careers is strictly rational and devoid of emotion.

Perhaps the deprecation of emotion and the praise of reason reflect a habit of mind. For the human mind seems to constantly partition the world into dualities: male and female, material and spiritual, nature and nurture, reason and emotion. But nature is not necessarily constituted of dualities. Such dichotomies prevent an understanding of the many continua and the integrated phenomena (such as a forest) that form so conspicuous a part of the living world.[7]

Even reason is part of a whole. It does not reside in a separate province of the mind that excludes emotion. The ability to reason depends on the ability to experience feelings. All our thinking includes emotion as well as reason. The presence of one does not mean the absence of the other. In particular, emotions and feelings are not intruders on the bastion of reason, they are enmeshed in its networks. Humans need to feel the world, to interact physically with it, in order to make any sense of it.

Perhaps in dismissing emotion, foresters and rationalists reveal their distrust and fear of love. For it is our loves that make life worth living, that hold us to this world and that illuminate and enliven it. In that sense, love, and those who love the world for its own sake, appear as the great enemy to those who wish to deny and destroy the world.

The powerful, and the agencies that do their bidding, cannot tolerate love of the world. Such attachments must be denied, denigrated and dismissed as emotion. Love of the forest is an obstacle to realising the foresters' dream of full utilisation. People's minds must be kept focused on the future utopia, on the rational future of wealth and abundance premised on the destruction of the forest. As far as those who direct CALM are concerned, people who oppose clearcutting are in the way—in the way of history, of progress and of development. They are classified and disposed of as obsolete and emotional. People so classified have to be defeated, beaten down, destroyed—just as the Luddites were overcome.

The Luddites were early-nineteenth-century English workers who opposed, often violently, the introduction of machinery that abolished their skills and their work lives. They opposed machinery 'destructive of commonality'. Luddites dared to stand in the way of progress, dared to assert the precedence of community needs and values over technological innovation and monetary profit. And they were dealt with, by the government and by industrialists, in a way that seems merely inevitable in the light of industrial civilisation's subsequent history.

The victory of industrialism over Luddism was overwhelming and unconditional: the most complete, significant and lasting victory of modern times. The decentralised, fairly independent local community in which the Luddites lived and worked was destroyed and absorbed by an aggressive, monetarily powerful, outside economy. The Luddites lost their community, their freedom, their jobs and in some cases their lives. Many were transported to Australia; others were hanged. Their children became the wage-earning servants of the victorious industrialists.

Industrialists not only won the ground war against the Luddites, they also won the propaganda war, the war fought in the realm of language and image. In the twentieth century, Luddism has become the most feared, the most crushing label that governments, their agencies and industry use to cower, humiliate and defeat the defenders of nature. Should any individual or group have the temerity to oppose the spread of technological destruction, they will be charged with Luddism, sedition and perhaps insanity.[8]

The charges are crippling. The state and the industrialists were so successful in suppressing the Luddite revolts and in vilifying machine breakers that Luddites have forever after been fixed in people's minds as the personifications of the opponents of technology and the antagonists of progress. And who cares to oppose progress? Yet, resisting the destruction of nature is not a manifestation of backwardness and has nothing to do with ignorance, as the victors over Luddism maintain. Nevertheless, conservationists take extraordinary care to avoid being labelled Luddites. Their circumspection renders their struggle for the conservation of nature ineffective.

And conservationists have been spectacularly unsuccessful. In the 25 years after the first Earth Day in 1970, humans reduced enough forests around the world to cover half of Australia, created enough desert to equal all the cropland in China and lost enough soil by other means—pavement and townhouses, wind and water erosion, inundation and chemical pollution—to equal all the cropland in India. During the same time, thousands of species became extinct, human population doubled and human appetites increased.

Carol and I walked down wide, open, shadeless Palings Road on a Sunday. Not a vehicle passed by except for a motorcycle, on which sat a young man and his girlfriend, who, waving and smiling, roared down the road and shortly after roared back. We walked east, and the hot afternoon sun bore down on our backs. After covering 12 kilometres, we rejoined the

Bibbulmun and turned south, back into the sheltering, cool bush, onto a track that followed Lefroy Brook.

A tributary of the Warren River, Lefroy Brook, like the Donnelly River, empties into the Southern Ocean. The eastern part of the Warren River catchment, the area of the Tone and Perup Rivers, is almost completely cleared. The Tone, especially, is saline, nutrient enriched and suffers eutrophication in the summer. Lefroy Brook forms the western part of the catchment and flows through forest and farmland. Although Warren River itself is undammed, private dams block so many tributaries that the river is one of the most segmented in the southwest. Diversions from the many small dams have significantly decreased the river's flow.

There are more than 100 000 private dams in the southwest. Many of them are small farm dams, dug into clay subsoils in cereal-growing areas and filled by paddock run-off. Generally these dams have little effect on streams and rivers. There are, however, hundreds of private gully dams. They inundate as much, or possibly more, river valley as the state-owned dams. Because they are usually surrounded by cleared land, they concentrate salt and nutrient pollution.

After an hour of following Lefroy Brook we reached the end of the day's walk. We had covered nearly 29 kilometres, the most we had walked in a single day on the whole trek. The Bibbulmun guidebook designated this point as stage 27A, but there was no sign that anyone had ever camped here before. A new logging road and bridge across Lefroy Brook, not shown on our maps, dissected the Bibbulmun track and obliterated 27A. But we were not going any farther. The day was late and storm clouds in the west promised rain. We cleared a patch of ground in the middle of the track and pitched the tent.

At dusk we built a small camp fire. Somewhere in the forest a boobook owl hooted. The clouds cleared and the sky brimmed with stars.

Overhead the planets in their courses about the sun made no sound. The earth was still. The moon rose. We had been in the bush, walking, for nearly one full lunar month. The moon had waned and waxed and was nearly full again.

The lunar cycle and the cycle of night and day are older than life on Earth. However, as far as many people are concerned, that does not mean the cycle cannot or should not be conquered. Early in 1993 scientists in Russia, using a thin aluminium and plastic mirror suspended in space, sent a narrow beam of reflected sunlight to the dark side of the earth. Many hailed the achievement as a great advance. Scaled up in size, proponents said, such a mirror could turn night into twilight at darker latitudes, thereby saving billions of dollars on electric lighting as well as extending planting and harvesting seasons.

Turning night into day would also constitute the most offensive form of pollution yet devised by humankind. Mirrors in space would erode the darkness that remains on this already overly incandescent planet, bleach the evening, turn midnight pale and blast away any surviving remnants of silence. It would also disrupt, perhaps end, the lives of the many animals and plants that regulate their lives by the length of day and night.

But if engineers and corporations find that turning night into day is more efficient, if it 'saves money', then the lives of circadian species will count for nothing. If a scheme somehow appeals to people as 'progress', then it will be implemented. Even a scheme as bizarre and untenable as mirrors in space could achieve unstoppable momentum in a matter of years. Opponents will be quickly, damnably and effectively dismissed as Luddites.

10

Money
answereth all

Rain started to fall soon after Carol and I went to bed at our camp by Lefroy Brook. Rain fell throughout the night but tapered off at dawn. We breakfasted and packed under clearing skies. Despite the previous day's marathon walk we quickly found our rhythm and followed the Waugals by the side of Lefroy Brook, around cleared grazing land and through cutover forest.

Some of the land beside the track had been cleared for farming more than 100 years ago. One farmer had cleared a large paddock, planted a few crops of wheat, then abandoned the land. A fire swept through the area. Karri seeds from nearby forest floated in, germinated and took root. Like all young karri trees, they grew quickly and reached 70 metres in 100 years. The regrowth now serves as a tourist attraction and forestry propaganda site.

CALM cites the 100 Year Old Forest to support its claims that regeneration quickly restores a clearcut. The claim is bogus, for there is no correspondence between what occurred 100 years ago and what occurs today. The original clearing took place in the midst of unbroken forest, unlike modern clearcuts. Moreover, the soil under this regrowth forest was not pummelled by log- and earth-moving machinery. Even more significant, the 100 Year Old Forest, with its grove of tall, straight, even-aged trees towering over a uniform and limited understorey, does not begin to approach the diversity, either in appearance or species mix, of an old-growth forest. Karri trees can live 500 years, not gaining much in height after the first 100 years but greatly increasing in girth and bulk. Several hundred more years of growth and decay, fire and flood, flux and stability would be required before this 100-year-old stand reproduces the conditions of old growth. In logged areas CALM will never permit trees to reach old growth.

As in the jarrah forest, CALM manages karri forest under multiple use, an inherently contradictory policy. Areas are managed according to a priority, such as recreation, conservation of flora, fauna and landscape, or wood production. This dual charge, to harmonise a mix of uses while preserving the biological integrity and aesthetics of the forest, is impossible. But foresters do not believe in conflicting or incompatible uses. They believe that wood production is compatible with almost every other management aim. Wood production is the priority in the greater part of the state forest. By 1986 CALM had allocated 90 400 hectares, or more than half of all the remaining publicly owned karri forest, to wood production.

The consequences of multiple use are the same as those of the disastrous logging policies of the past: degradation and extinction. Mammals and birds became endangered, and some extinct, in the southwest forests within a few years of the start of large-scale logging: Gilbert's potoroo (extinct around 1900), the rufous bushbird (last seen in 1906) and

Lewin's rail (last seen in 1931). Local extinctions were widespread, such as the woylie and the numbat from the Blackwood plateau. Birds that were once relatively widespread retreated to smaller ranges. These include the western bristlebird, noisy scrub bird and western whipbird. The ground parrot and the mallee fowl have also nearly disappeared from the forest.

Many presently endangered species continue to decline as a consequence of logging: the chuditch, numbat, woylie, tammar wallaby and yellow-bellied frog. Once common mammals are now uncommon: the brush-tailed possum, brush wallaby, quokka, water rat and brush-tailed tuan.

The decline in actual diversity in the forest parallels a decline in appreciation of diversity in general. Previous generations had a deep and abiding fascination with variance, difference and miscellany. Their love of diversity was the love of the specific and the unique.

The spirit that moved Botticelli to incorporate at least 30 different species of plants in his canvas *Spring*, painted in 1478, has been impaired; the spirit that inspired Shakespeare to mention enough animal and plant species in his plays to provide source material for entire books and suggestions for complete gardens has been effectively sublimated; the spirit that animated indefatigable Baron Ferdinand von Mueller to assemble a huge collection of Australian flora has been suppressed; the spirit that possessed squatter Edward M. Curr and gave him the energy and determination to compile his great collection of comparative vocabularies of 214 different Aboriginal languages has been devalued; and the spirit that vivified Georgiana Molloy and led her to discover an all-consuming passion amid the floristic richness of the southwest has been stifled. This once spacious and abundant spirit, if not entirely vanished, has been cramped and corrupted in our day.

The decline of the love of diversity parallels the decline in diversity itself. In both cases the cause is the same—the ascendancy of diversity's opposite: uniformity. The modern world has abandoned previous generations' fascination with the specific, with species, with individual difference, in favour of a preoccupation with the general and the generalisable.

Foresters, economists, in fact most modern professionals, find the complexity of life, the particular and the specific, unmanageable. Categories, however, are tractable. Categories make the reconstruction of the forest easier. Foresters intent on remaking the forest into a plantation need to ignore the specific, the individual and the unique in order to concentrate on the generalisable and the manipulable. As professional managers, foresters prefer categories and reductions to the idiosyncratic and individual.

CALM contends that logging in the karri forest is based on a 100-year rotation. Accordingly, the area logged each year should not exceed one-hundredth of the total area allocated to wood production. This amount is consistently exceeded, often by huge amounts.

In only one year (1983) between 1977 and 1985 was the area logged equal to or less than the area that should have been logged. Since then overcutting has continued. In 1992, the year before Carol and I walked the Bibbulmun, CALM reported 1850 hectares of karri cut, twice the one-hundredth limit. In 1993 1440 hectares was logged—again, greatly in excess of the sustainable amount.[1]

More karri forest is being logged than the forest can sustain if a steady output is desired. But this is not CALM's aim. Sustained yield no longer means what it once did. It has come to represent more a theoretical than an empirical approach to forestry. Actual measurements of growth increment in the real forest have become less important than theoretical calculations of the growing capacity of fully regulated plantations. CALM sees natural forests, old-growth forests, as impediments to sustained yield. The sooner the old forest is removed, the sooner the theoretical replacement plantations can begin to yield theoretical sustained production.

From the 100 Year Old Forest the Bibbulmun descended to swampy ground. Carol and I sloshed through puddles and stepped across two small side streams flowing into Lefroy Brook. The track followed the boundary of private land, most of it cleared for pasture. In the state forest a small side stream had been dammed to form Big Brook Dam. We stopped at the picnic area to eat. A flock of magpies descended, anticipating sharing the food. They were disappointed. A cold, light shower fell, and we decided to resume walking, but not on the Bibbulmun. Although the Bibbulmun led straight to Pemberton, only 7 kilometres away, we planned to follow the Warren circuit to Stirling Road and from there walk to Pimelea Youth Hostel, where we hoped to spend the night.

The Warren circuit followed tourist drives through the karri forest. After a few kilometres of gravel track we arrived at the junction with paved Stirling Road, turned north, and early in the afternoon reached the hostel, a collection of huts and cottages, once a forestry settlement. No one was about. We ate lunch, inspected the accommodations and decided to move on.

Pemberton was 10 kilometres down Stirling Road. We put out our thumbs, but the few cars that passed ignored us. We started walking. Several kilometres later a mid-1960 Holden station wagon pulled over. We flung our packs into the back and settled them among jarrah boards, wood shavings and woodworking tools.

The driver, Tom, was a cabinet and furniture maker, working primarily with reclaimed jarrah: old fence posts, mill ends, salvaged building timber and logging discards. He wore a Save the Hawke Block badge.

'What's the Hawke Block?' we asked.

He explained that it comprised the last stands of virgin karri forest in the Pemberton area. West of the town and located between Warren National Park and the Warren River, the 3290-hectare forest had been designated a wood production priority area by CALM. Eighty percent of the block was scheduled for clearcutting, most of it for woodchips.

The Save the Hawke Block badge, which, Tom said, we would see many more of in Pemberton, was part of the effort by the local Warren Environmental Group (WEG) and the West Australian Forest Alliance (WAFA) to preserve the area. Besides the old-growth karri, which included a grove of big trees and some of the oldest known karri trees still standing, the Hawke Block contained uncut jarrah forest, Warren River cedar woodlands and rare stands of pure marri. It was also home to several rare and endangered animals, including the western ringtail possum, uncommon quokka, short-nosed snake, square-nosed snake and Dells skink.

A 116-hectare coupe had already been clearfelled. Since then, CALM had pushed extra logging roads through the forest. In protest WEG and WAFA had organised rallies and road blocks and had seeded the recently bulldozed roads. More protests and rallies were planned.[2]

'CALM,' Tom said, 'never saw a tree it didn't want to cut down or a forest it didn't want to clearfell.'

Tom dropped us off at the Pemberton Tourist Office. Inside, the officer behind the counter wore a Save the Hawke Block badge. Although an intense passion seemed ignited at the mention of the Hawke Block, he was reluctant to talk about the forest while on duty. We picked up brochures on forest and mill tours given by Bunnings and obtained directions to Warren Lodge.

The town of Pemberton lies on either side of one long main street, the Vasse Highway, with the Bunnings timber mill at the lower end and shops and garages at the other. Warren Lodge, which included a large house and a barracks building—once the single men's quarters for millworkers—was opposite the mill. A young couple, Chloe and Chris, leased the buildings from Bunnings and ran the house as a bed and breakfast and the barracks as a backpackers' hostel. They told us that Charlotte, the woman walking the Bibbulmun on her own, had stayed at the hostel a few weeks earlier.

We took a room in the barracks. The hostel's only other guests, a family from New South Wales, were touring the southwest by car.

This day we had walked a long way, and we looked forward to rest. But instead of owl hoots and wind stirring in forest branches at night, we heard the incessant roar and rumble of the mill relentlessly devouring timber until 1.00 a.m. Birds called through the still of the dawn. But in a few minutes the mill started up again.

Late in the morning we walked into town, bought some groceries and ate lunch at Chloe's restaurant. A petition seeking the conservation of the Hawke Block lay on the counter. We signed.

Several dozen woodworkers, sculptors, potters, painters, basket-weavers and other craftspeople live in and around Pemberton. Workshops and studios display their wares. One studio, Fine Woodcraft, owned and operated by Murray and Lillian Johnson, was a work of art in itself. Most of the timber in the building, including the main supports, consisted of mill rejects. Doors and architraves had been milled and carved from karri, to prove, Murray said, that karri was a fine woodworking timber, suited to better use than woodchips. The Johnsons' merchandise included wood furniture, wood knick-knacks, ceramics and jewellery. Most of the woodcraft had been made from salvaged or recycled timber. Murray hoped that eventually all his stock would be from salvaged or recycled timber.

He spoke about the Hawke Block, clearcutting and CALM's deception. CALM, he said, was a subsidiary of Bunnings, striving always to extract more and more timber from the forest. Recently CALM had proposed that a new powerline through the southwest should be built with a kilometre-wide clearance. This was much wider than usual. The extra clearing would yield timber for Bunnings. CALM had also proposed cutting the timber from roadside edges, also for Bunnings.

The similarity of interest between CALM and the timber industry (that is, Bunnings) was further shown by the fact that their separate submissions to independent inquiries tended to be identical. They separately, but indistinguishably, objected to any measure limiting industry access to 'resources' (trees are always designated as 'resources'). And they consistently supported intensified logging.[3]

CALM (like the former Forests Department) opposed the conservation of jarrah and karri forest. Reasons never varied. Foresters claimed that it was unacceptable to impose any limit on the availability of hardwood. Conservation would disrupt the southwest timber industry (Bunnings) and unbalance the extraction of wealth.

To expose CALM's masquerade that regrowth following clearcutting soon resembled true forest, Murray urged us to visit the 100 Year Old Forest and then the old-growth forest in Warren National Park. The difference, he said, could not be clearer. You did not have to be a naturalist to notice the greater abundance and diversity of both animal and plant life in the true old-growth forest.

We later heard Murray make a similar and equally impassioned recommendation to another couple in the store. He spent more time talking about conservation than he did about his merchandise. We complimented him on his energy and commitment. He said he was engaged in 'education' and that when customers chided him about being a Greenie, he responded that he was a businessman selling timber products who had an interest in saving the forest for other uses.

Murray said that tourism, for example, was much more important economically than logging. In Pemberton alone—founded as a mill town—Bunnings employed 100 people; the local tourist industry employed more than 300. But the timber industry was organised, wealthy and influential. The southwest tourist industry, in contrast, lacked a collective voice.

Carol and I heard the tourism argument from many other people in Pemberton. But I wondered whether they really had their heart in it. More likely, the circumstances of public debate in Australia force them to justify preservation on economic grounds. In a market culture, non-economic, non-utilitarian justifications lack legitimacy. Conservationists, therefore, employ utility to justify, what are, in reality, moral feelings towards the natural world. Do they really believe their own arguments? They certainly appear to believe that utilitarian arguments persuade other people. But how can people get passionate about utility? How can abstractions such as development, sustainability and productivity generate as much care and concern as actual life: trees, soil, rivers, flowers, animals?

Utilitarian arguments are insufficient because they are self-defeating. What if the Hawke Block fails to attract tourists? What if no wonderful pharmaceutical products can be cultured from its gene pool? What if most of the natural world proves useless to human purposes? Are we then free to destroy?

The justification for preservation on the basis of the preserved species' utility applies only as long as a better use for the space currently occupied by the preserved species or forest is not found. Once that use is discovered and, inevitably, with the growth in human numbers and appetites, it will be, then preservation loses its rationale. Utility leads only to destruction. Utility leads to an impoverished world with no room for non-useful species.

In any case, I did not believe that the people fighting for the Hawke Block formed barricades because they believe that the forest has tourist potential or utility. Protestors lie in front of bulldozers because they are fighting for the life of the forest, because they love the forest and because they believe the forest is beautiful. Yet, a general unwillingness, indeed an embarrassment, to argue explicitly for their passion undercuts their cause.

To be truly convincing, nature lovers must reject language that disguises affection for the natural world. Otherwise nature remains speechless—the land erodes, salt spreads, forests fall, soil acidity rises, species die, biotas disintegrate and climates wobble.

There is only one way to halt destruction. There is only one way to give voice to nature. Nature lovers must argue with honesty. They must argue something less egotistic, less anthropocentric, less economic and more emphatic. The first argument for conservation must be ethical: plants and animals, and the order of nature to which they belong, have a right to exist and be left alone because they exist. The earth does not belong to us.

From Fine Woodcraft Carol and I walked to the Forest Industries building. The woman at the desk invited us to join a mill tour. With about twenty other people we first watched a CALM video that praised the wonderful job that foresters were doing in managing the forests. The woman in charge then gave a short speech extolling the virtues of the 100 Year Old Forest. She did not confirm what we had heard earlier: that although logs cut from old farm areas often contain nails that damage the saws, the greatest source of damage was Waugal signs. She did say, however, 'We don't cut down a single tree unless authorised by CALM.'

She sounded like an economist. Her presentation was flat and programmed. Perhaps she had been instructed by the public relations office at Bunnings to be unemotional, perhaps she had given the presentation too many times, or perhaps she did not consider herself married to the Bunnings' way of life and saw no reason to put any feeling into her job. Whatever the reasons, the audience was unmoved and possibly, in some quarters at least, sceptical.

We donned hard-hats and followed our guide to the mill. She led us up steel stairs to a metal walkway high above the saws, tables, conveyors and assembly lines packed into a vast metal-clad shed. Outside, loader machines lifted karri logs onto conveyors. The rollers turned and the logs, wrapped with chains, entered the building. Metal arms jiggled the logs across conveyors, loosened the chains and drove the logs irresistibly into giant saw blades. As the sawdust flew, it was impossible not to think of the mill as a slaughterhouse. Carol felt sick.

The Pemberton mill is one of Bunnings' biggest and most efficient. Yet only about 40 percent of the logs that enter it are converted to sawn timber. The residue is shipped to the Bunnings chip mill in Manjimup. But the logs that come into Pemberton mill represent forest residue to begin with. Nearly 70 percent of all clearfelled karri and marri logs go straight to the chipper. Thus, some 85 percent of all the timber in the karri forest ends up chipped.

During the first 17 years of woodchipping, to 1993, twice as much karri forest had been felled for woodchips than was cleared for agriculture in the previous 140 years. Twelve-and-a-half million tonnes of karri and marri trees had been chipped and sent to Japan to be made into paper products and ultimately discarded. The woodchip industry laid waste to the forest to make rubbish.

Late in the afternoon Carol and I bought groceries and returned to the backpackers. Unlike the previous night, the hostel was now full. Most guests, however, went out for dinner and did not compete for the single hotplate in the hostel's kitchen. We talked to an American cyclist, Don, from southern California. He had cycled long distances in North America and Europe. He now planned to bike across the Nullarbor.

Rain fell during the night and partly muffled the sound of the mill. The air inside the barracks was close and still. We slept uneasily.

Next morning we walked out of town to the Gloucester Tree, Pemberton's most popular tourist attraction. At 61 metres, the fire lookout on top of the old karri is reputed to be the highest tree-mounted lookout in the world. We climbed the steel rungs that spiralled around the trunk. From the top we looked over the undulating crowns of a forest broken by sawmills, roads and clearings. Behind us a party of schoolchildren started the ascent. Several of them panicked halfway up and had to be coaxed down by their teachers. More children started the climb as we descended, so that there were now some two dozen people crawling around the tree. We reached the ground just as a cloudburst dropped a heavy shower of rain. From a shelter we watched the bedraggled children in the tree hang on to the slippery rails.

During dinner that night at the hostel two English tourists turned on the television. Since the hostel had one small common area that served as kitchen, dining room, living room and television lounge, the blaring television instantly dominated the space and immobilised communal talk and interaction. Yet, the couple did not watch what they had turned on. I asked them to turn the television off. They turned the volume down but said they must have the set on so they would not miss a show coming on later.

Their addiction to television highlighted a perhaps insurmountable obstacle to conservation of the world. True conservation (not wise use) asks people to be still, to be quiet, to listen. But television has destroyed these meditative forms of existence. Television creates a fantasy world full of dulling stimulation. Habitual television viewers would find it difficult to stand still in a forest, attentive and listening: sunsets would be too slow, moon rises excruciatingly prolonged. The pace of nature would be interminable, pointless, boring.

In a fast-paced world people lose the capacity to respond to the degradation of the earth. In the built-up, enclosed world of cities, where everything has been formed for human purpose, people have minimal experience of natural things and are detached from nature. In these circumstances conservation faces a whole constellation of obstacles. The easiest to recognise is opposition from people who oppose the keeping of wildness for reasons of wealth. These people would shape the world into an open-cut mine and a clearcut forest. Yet they control government, CALM, industry, education, media and most of the country's civic institutions.

But the wealthy and the powerful may not be the most potent opposition to conservation. There is another block of humanity that simply does not care and an unsorted group who think of themselves as conservationists and who, in one way or another, are. These people advocate saving nature for crops, meat, water, wood, picnic grounds, recreation and as material for study in laboratories. Putting this mixture of motives and aspirations together under the label *conservation* has made, in some cases, a temporarily stronger front. But the alliance does not face the really tough obligation at all. It has muddied the real issue, hidden the dimensions of the enormous job and kept everybody from articulating the awful certainty that conservation must exist for the sake of nature itself.

No significant preserving of the natural world can be done with slight sacrifice. The true test will come when great sacrifices are needed, when it becomes necessary to fight the indifference of most of the urban world, the active opposition of much of it and to surmount the culture's determination to disconnect human existence from nature.[4]

11

Things holy, profane, clean, obscene, grave and light

Words are never neutral. All words have origins, pre-existing meanings and biased associations. The use of words in language is constraining as well as liberating. Language fixes and channels patterns of thought in predetermined ways.

Yet, although words entrap, thought itself does not depend on words. If the brain thought exclusively in words, how could we possibly think as fast as we do? Words provide precision, enabling us to give the brain tasks and to scrutinise and articulate an essentially subconscious thinking process. Thus, words, while not conferring an ability to think, give us an ability to direct our thoughts. And here they are indispensable.

In thinking about the forest, we can hardly escape the need to speak of *ecology* and *ecosystems*. But the terms are biased, they betray their origins and they predispose users to see reality in certain ways. *Ecology* and *ecosystem* come from the abstract, rational intellectuality of the universities and have been invented to disconnect, displace and disembody the mind.

The prefix *ec-* in the words *ecology* and *economics* derives from the Greek *oikos*, meaning house or home. The compound *economy* is also of Greek origin and referred to someone who managed a household, more specifically a steward. Therefore *economics* implies housekeeping or the management of the home.[1]

The word *ecology* was coined by Ernst Haeckel, a nineteenth-century German populariser of evolutionary theory. Haeckel combined *oikos* and the Greek *logos*, meaning word, speech, discourse or reason. Strictly speaking, then, *ecology* might refer to a discourse about the home—home, in this sense meaning the earth. Haeckel, however, had a more specific and technical use for the term. *Ecology* described the study of organic diversity and the interactions of organisms and their surroundings in order to address what may be the most fundamental question in evolutionary biology: Why are there so many kinds of living things?[2]

To extend the metaphor of the word's origins and its cognates, ecology concerns the economy of the great house of nature. Ecology seeks to reveal nature's structure in space and time and especially the interactions of animals and plants with themselves and with one another. The word spelled a recognition that the proper study of life is neither the individual or the species but the whole of life, seen in all its combinations, dwellings and niches.

The word *ecosystem* combines *oikos* and *system*. System is a notion culled from the history of technology and of machines. System implies structure, building and regulation, all machinelike attributes. Ecosystem implies that the house of nature is a machine—a machine of many interrelated parts to be sure, but a machine nonetheless. Descriptions of the world that include the word *ecosystem* reflect and reinforce modern, mechanistic prejudices. Such descriptions also reflect the etymology and the rules of language. They do not reflect nature.

The usefulness and the limits of the word *ecosystem* demonstrate how, through language, nature is revealed to us and how also, through language, nature is transformed into material, into resources, into a machine.

Stories add another layer of prejudice and bias to words, often rendering the bias stronger and more immune to disclosure. Most modern stories celebrate progress. Under the progressive perception of reality— the perception that has informed most Australian storytelling—nature is seen as disorderly; humans, in contrast, are seen as orderly. This perceived discrepancy, this disjunction, invites Australians to impose their order and orderliness on the unruly continent by means of taming, conquering and managing the natural world.

Forestry and the timber industry, like broadscale monoculture and mining (which in Australia are little different), always promote themselves as rousing successes. Success is celebrated in the stories foresters tell: stories of progress that proceed from the dark days of inefficiency and waste into the clear light of the present 'uneven flow sustained yield'.

CALM foresters, for example, see the passage of the Forests Act in 1918 and the establishment of the Forests Department in 1919 in terms of progress. Science and rationality overcame ignorance and irrationality. The Forests Department came into existence out of a struggle between enlightenment and superstition, between scientific management and shortsighted politicians and entrenched timber interests. CALM's P.E.S. Christensen, who takes up the story after Charles Lane-Poole's appointment in 1919, writes:

> Thus began an epic three-way struggle between Lane-Poole, a strong and articulate advocate for forestry, Sir James Mitchell, the then Premier and

staunch proponent for agriculture, and the timber industry, which for long had had its own way. Lane-Poole's resignation in 1922 was perhaps an inevitable result of his outspoken style and fierce concern for the forest. However, the battle once joined was carried on in just as able, but perhaps more tenacious, if less heroic, style by his successor Stephen L. Kessell.[3]

Christensen writes in the progressive tradition shared by most modern historians. For progressives, the human story is one of steady improvement, of progress towards enlightenment and rationality. Modern historians, both of the left and the right, regard industrial civilisation as both necessary and inevitable. Most historians side with the victors in the war against Luddism. They disseminate a view that life without an industrial economy is virtually impossible. Their stories consist of a series of fictions about the misery of existence before the invention of the steam engine and the defeat of the Luddites.

Among the machinery remaining from early industrial logging in the Pemberton area is a tramway. Restored as a tourist attraction, it runs 30 kilometres between Pemberton and Northcliffe. Carol and I had sent our third and last food box to Northcliffe and so decided to cover the route by tram.

Our third morning in Pemberton dawned showery and cool. The forecast called for clearing, fine weather; the overcast sky suggested otherwise. We were the first up at the backpackers' hostel but were soon joined at breakfast by three builders staying at the hostel while working in Pemberton.

We put in a load of laundry and hung the clothes out with an eye on the weather. The rain held off. We packed, hoisted on our packs and walked down a road bordered by weatherboard cottages, each with a load of firewood in the front yard.

At the tramway station we boarded one of several open carriages behind a small diesel locomotive. The carriages filled quickly with tourists disembarking from buses and cars. The tram left mid-morning, crossed the Vasse Highway, rounded the Bunnings timber mill and headed south into the bush. The driver gave a running commentary on the history and botany of the area. In a few kilometres we crossed the main branch of the Warren River. Its tea-coloured waters flowed between banks bordered by wattie (*Agonis juniperina*), a tall shrub of the karri forest that grows in very moist areas, and by large marri trees, which grow to a massive size along the Warren River. With the exception of the very central portion of the forest, karri occurs in mixtures, in association with woodlands, heath-lands and sedgelands. The tramway passed through all these forest types and low-lying flat areas covered in swampy heath with a rich mixture of bottlebrushes: melaleucas, beaufortias, callistemons and a host of myrtles.

Our driver stopped frequently, and most of the passengers, carrying expensive cameras mounted with macro lenses, got out to photograph the numerous and beautiful wildflowers growing near the tramway embank-ment. Hillocks, covered with stunted jarrah–marri forest, rose from the swamps. Trees grew taller at the top, making the ridges more conspicuous.

The journey was noisy, smelly (of diesel fumes) and cold and grew colder as we approached Northcliffe. Carol and I snuggled down behind the sides of the carriage, out of the wind. We could see Waugal signs nailed to trees where the Bibbulmun followed the railway. At Northcliffe the tram pulled into a siding next to the tourist office and opposite the main street, lined on one side with a few buildings: hardware store, supermarket, hotel, worm farm, general store and restaurant. All the passengers, who were returning to Pemberton on the tram in an hour's time, sought warmth and food. Carol and I walked to the caravan park, where we took an on-site van for the night.

Back in town we ordered lunch at the Hollow Butt Restaurant. Pro-gun propaganda and Christian messages were pinned to the wall. The homemade food was good and hearty. Afterwards we walked the length of the town, shopped at the supermarket, picked up our food parcel from the post office (in the local service station) and visited the tourist office and pioneer museum. The museum housed artefacts (tools, furnishings, kitchenware) and displays (a milking shed, period schoolroom) from the 1920s and celebrated the era when the Northcliffe area was first cleared and broken for agriculture.

In 1920 Western Australia's premier, James Mitchell, proposed a scheme to conquer the karri. In the forest's place he wanted to see dairy farms built through Group Settlement, an idea derived from the victory of the machine in the Great War. 'The war,' according to a contemporary, 'had provided an object lesson in the power of organised bodies of men to surmount physical obstacles before which, as individuals, they would have stood helpless.' Inspired by the words and metaphors of war, Mitchell planned a mass attack against the forest, mounted by settlers deployed in units of 20 men under the command of a foreman for each 64-hectare homestead block. Groups received orders to clear an area of 2 hectares for intense cultivation and to partly clear an additional 8 hectares for pasture, as well as dig drains, run out fences and erect outbuildings and dwellings.[4]

To clear the forest, settlers used explosives and tree-pulling machines. But most settlers were urban immigrants from Britain and were inexperienced at clearing land. Removing the immense hardwood trees proved exceedingly difficult. At the rate of destroying one tree in four days, clearing even 2 hectares took a very long time. Groups quickly abandoned complete clearing in favour of ringbarking. But ringbarked trees took two or more years to die. Moreover, when cleared, much of the land proved poor, deficient in minerals, waterlogged in winter and sour where heavy timber had been uprooted by chains or explosives.

Blocks were successively deserted and reoccupied by inexperienced newcomers. In the meantime, settlers were sustained by state grants and loans. Expenses mounted, debts grew, everyone complained. The scheme was suspended, refinanced, resumed, abandoned. Fewer than half the number of farms planned were eventually established.

But the planners and politicians did not despair. If group settlement destroyed tens of thousands of hectares of forest, turned the soil sour and created a community permanently in debt, that was a sign of great things to come. Optimism—the belief underlying rationalism's faith that a better society could be built on the ruins of the present—had taken up permanent residence in the minds of leading men.

Mitchell had promised the group settlers that all they had to do to realise a life just like the one they were leaving (but far more prosperous) was to clear the native vegetation and bring in the plough. The promise was bogus, but Mitchell lived in an age of optimism, an era of promises.

In the 1920s foresters, doctors, scientists, politicians and advertisers promised a future of efficiency. Human technical prowess—management—would transform the course of life into a predictable pursuit of personal wellbeing. While foresters might disagree with agriculturalists over the disposal of the forest, they did agree on the broader aims of management: to subject all life to factorylike standards of efficiency. Trees, milk, consumer goods, even happiness, were to be turned out like automobiles off an assembly line. Advocates of efficiency advanced the industrialisation of life within the context of a key idiom promoted by the

Great War and summarised in the newly fashionable word *system*—life was a machine. Although the group settlers, wet and cold, toiling in the muck and morass of their cleared lots, may not have realised it, they were part of a system. Western Australia's planners conceived of Group Settlement as a system and as a systematic attempt to eradicate the forest.

From the pioneer museum Carol and I returned to the caravan, unpacked the food parcel and distributed the contents between our two packs. The forecast continued to call for clearing weather, but next morning dawned dark. Heavy cumulus clouds hung low in the sky. We walked into the village, where road workers, noting our packs, guessed our intentions and told us that the forecast now called for thunder and heavy rain. They predicted we were 'in for a wet old hike'. Carol argued that walking under such conditions was not a wise move. We left anyway.

Outside the village we rejoined the Bibbulmun, which now tended easterly. The sky opened. The rain, driven by a strong westerly wind, pelted down. Our ponchos flapped in the wind. Water ran down our necks and splashed against our legs and into our boots. Never before on the Bibbulmun had we encountered such heavy rain. Surging, muddy brown rivulets ran along either side of the track, a connected series of farm roads that skirted paddock and bush. The rain poured down without pause. At a small corrugated iron depository for milk cans, we took shelter. The rain drummed against the iron and water dripped onto our heads through numerous nail holes.

With the aid of our map, we calculated distances and studied the route ahead. The track continued through a mosaic of cleared land and remnant bush. The prospect did not appeal. It was not, we reasoned, worth getting soaked for. We were hiking to see the forest, not farmland. Yet, until the Bibbulmun entered Shannon National Park, about 25 kilometres ahead, it passed through larger and larger tracts of cleared country. We decided to get to Shannon National Park more directly, by returning to Northcliffe and hitching.

We stepped outside our leaky shelter onto Boorara Road, which led straight to Northcliffe. We had walked barely 300 metres when a pick-up truck appeared, the first vehicle we had seen all day. It stopped, and three young farm workers in the front welcomed us aboard. Carol and I climbed into the back and crouched down among shovels and baling twine. Cold wind and rain whipped around and over the cabin as we sped into Northcliffe.

We stopped outside the tourist office and went straight to the wood stove, where we spent an hour warming up, drying out and chatting with the attendant, Shashi. We then walked across the road to the Hollow Butt Restaurant. Carol spoke to a couple who had been on yesterday's tram. They were driving to Shannon and offered us a lift—if we could fit in with our packs. We squeezed our packs in among golf clubs and luggage.

Lloyd and Dorothy, from Sandringham, Victoria, were nearly retired and had spent several weeks touring Western Australia in their Commodore. Lloyd was a member of Rotary, and wherever he travelled he looked for potential luncheon speakers. Perhaps we could talk about the Bibbulmun and the environment?

'You must be environmentalists,' he said.

'No, we're nature lovers.'

'Aren't they the same thing?'

'No, they represent two entirely different outlooks.'

Words entrap. *Environment* is a weighted and biased term that disconnects us from the world. These disconnections stem from the word's history.

French Enlightenment scientists emphasised the concept of environment. It was, after all, a French word and meant that which surrounds and encircles. Étienne Saint-Hilaire (1772–1844) observed: 'The environment is all powerful in modifying organized bodies.' In this sense *environment* referred to external influences. It meant a world separate from and outside of organisms.

Jean Baptiste Pierre Antoine de Monet le Chevalier de Lamarck (1744–1829) also emphasised environment and externality:

> The environment affects the shape and organisation of animals, that is to say that when the environment becomes very different, it produces in the course of time corresponding modifications in the shape and organization of animals.[5]

Following Saint-Hilaire, Lamarck and other French writers, the word *environment* entered the English language. Charles Darwin (1809–82) did not agree with Lamarck that the environment and its changes were the primary instigators of evolution. For Darwin, random variation (intrinsic to organisms) was present first, and the ordering activity of the environment (natural selection) followed. Nevertheless, Darwin embraced the word and found the concept crucial to his view of life.

Darwin used *environment* to denote the conditions of nature that determined an organism's chance of survival. But Darwin's definition was imprecise and implicit rather than explicit. The word evolved: whereas, at first, *environment* had a restricted sense and applied to immediate circumstances, it gradually came to refer to more and more of nature, until *environment* included the entire living world.

This mixed, even contradictory, meaning is part of the word's legacy and is inherent in its modern use. Nevertheless, ambiguity has not lessened its attractiveness. As a scientific term in general use, *environment* lends scientific legitimacy, rectitude and pretension to the discussions in which it is employed. But *environment*, like *ecology* and *ecosystem*, is a word subject to the vagaries and fashions of science. Rather than describing the world, *environment* ratifies the world view of science. Users of the word become partners in the greater project of science—the conquest of nature.

The bias towards conquest is reflected in the word's intrinsic instrumentality. *Environment* has come to mean an arena of operation and influence, sometimes reciprocal, sometimes not. In particular, *environment* refers to an arena for human activity, as in the DOS environment, an airconditioned environment, the educational environment. These environments challenge humans to take charge. Environments exist for human use.

This instrumental outlook is imposed on nature when the environment and the natural world are considered synonymous. But nature is not the environment. Compared with the environment, nature is much more formidable. Nature resists manipulation.

Etymology also reflects the fact that the environment is not nature. Like *environment*, the word *nature* has a history, but one that is richer, more venerable and ancient. *Nature* has roots in Indo-European, Greek and Latin words that all mean 'to be born'. The modern cognate of those roots, *nature*, refers to the whole living world, to a natural world that came into being without the help of humans.

Nature's associations are pagan, not technical or mechanistic. Nature is more than the environment, it is more than us. Nature runs through us, and it discourages possession. Although we speak of 'our environment', we could never say 'our nature'.

Environments are technologies, products of science. As a reduction of nature, *the environment* is useful to managers and engineers. The term permits them to advocate environmental management. *Environment* encourages the engineering compulsion to systematically adjust and readjust the world. Saving the environment is reduced to a technical undertaking. Such advocacy does not appear quite so legitimate when applied to nature. To suggest that we must take care in an unenvironed world, a world that came into being without human assistance, sounds inexact, unscientific, mystical even. Environments, in contrast, are perfect foils for the modern urge to control and conquer. Engineers, informed by science, can manage an environment in a way they cannot manage nature. This is why the modern world prefers *environment* to *nature*. *Environment* reduces nature to an arena for control.

Much of the planning behind control takes place at universities, and it invariably relates to environment. When in schools of environmental studies students talk excitedly of becoming 'environmental managers', engineers talk of computer-assisted plans to drain salinised land and economists explain how market forces, operating according to the laws of supply and demand, will clear the air of pollution, rid the atmosphere of ozone-depleting chemicals, save native forests, preserve the Great Barrier Reef and restore rivers and waterways, they are all referring to the environment and to human benefit. No one attends to nature.

For example, according to Professor Jorg Imberger, of the University of Western Australia's Centre for Water Research, 'Environmental engineers are people who will possess the technical skills to design a new way of living on our planet.' Upon examination, however, it is obvious that the 'new way of living' that Professor Imberger envisages is no different from present ways of living and depends utterly on conventional bureaucratic and commercial arrangements that perpetuate and profit from human destructiveness and disregard for nature.

Imberger believes that his centre's mission 'is to create new ideas'. But these ideas apply only in the context of 'the global market place'. Subject to 'a major marketing exercise', they must be compatible with managerial imperatives and evolve in the context of 'globalisation'. 'In effect,' he continues, 'we will be offering our wares to large international companies.' Such ideas, or 'wares', cannot, of course, question that marketplace and the ways of living it gives rise to.[6]

As universities embrace globalisation, they forfeit the ability and the will to think. Research centres like Professor Imberger's downgrade thought to management and address questions of a very narrow kind—those congruent with the interests of transnational corporations.

As centres of progressivism, universities are in the grip of a paralysing fatalism that informs the whole discourse of progress, growth and wealth. For example, politicians, business people and academics who argue in favour of population increase or immigration or who simply argue that Australia has no choice but to accept immigrants, and that population increase and immigration are inevitable, display a remarkable passivity and acquiescence with respect to human demands. They regard human demands as inexorable, always increasing, inevitable, unchangeable, almost sacred.

Advocates of growth see the non-human world as plastic and endlessly adaptable to human demands. 'The environment', they believe, can be forced to accommodate an indefinite expansion of the human enterprise. Such beliefs display an extraordinary fatalism with respect to growth and technology and an extraordinary credulity with respect to the planet's capacity to accommodate human demands.

12

Countenance
silence

Lloyd and Dorothy drove us to South Western Highway and the abandoned mill town of Shannon. Now a camping and caravan area with an
amenities block and golf course within Shannon National Park, Shannon
Mill operated from 1948 to 1970. Most of the town was then dismantled.
Only foundations, compacted earth and the exotic plants that accompany
all mill towns remain. The Bibbulmun once ended at Shannon, but not
anymore. Carol and I still had nearly 100 kilometres to walk before we
reached Walpole.

A CALM ranger at Northcliffe had recommended the hikers' huts at
Shannon campground as excellent shelter. With the day continuing wet,
we intended to take his advice. At the main camping area a few caravans
sat under dripping trees off a circular road. On nearby grassy slopes
several tents flapped in the wind. Outside the toilet and shower block a
pile of firewood, a chopping block and an axe stood near a do-it-yourself
wood-fired boiler. We explored a couple of the adjacent single-room huts.

In one, the pot-belly stove was alight, but the bunks held no gear. We concluded the hut was unoccupied and decided to stay. Rain began again, heavy and continual.

We read the hut book and noted the comments from tourists, campers and hikers. Several thanked CALM for providing the huts and congratulated the agency for 'doing something constructive instead of destructive for a change'.

Shortly there was a knock at the door. A man carrying a billy entered. John claimed responsibility for the fire. He was not staying in the hut—he had a caravan—but wished to provide warmth and conviviality for the eventual occupier. He put the billy on the stove and later returned for tea with his wife, Barbara. They were from Tasmania and were touring Australia. They liked the Shannon area and had stayed several days. John had split a lot of firewood, for both the shower block boiler and the hut.

He told us that Don, the American cyclist whom Carol and I had met at Warren Lodge, was staying in another hut. Don then appeared at the door and joined us for tea. He had ridden to Shannon that morning, after having spent two nights in Northcliffe nursing a bad knee. He wondered whether he had the stamina, determination and leg power to make the trip across the Nullarbor.

Except for a few short periods, rain fell throughout the afternoon. A young woman with two small sons dropped by. She said that while her husband and a friend were putting up their tent, she and her sons wanted to warm their hands by the stove.

Rain and hail continued through the night. There were no more social visits. Carol and I sat in the dark around the warm stove. Occasionally the moon shone through cloud breaks, and soft light poured through the hut's window. Vehicles kept arriving at the campground. One drove up to our door to check if the hut was empty. At midnight the searching light from the torch of another unbedded party flashed briefly into the hut.

In the morning John reported that the weather forecast predicted showers but clearing through Sunday and Monday. It had been a cold night. Perth had recorded a low of 3 degrees Celsius, and snow had fallen on the Porongorups.

Today Carol and I planned a short walk of less than 10 kilometres, so we were in no hurry to leave. After porridge and a shower we walked to South Western Highway and crossed to a pavilion that had sheltered three groups overnight. We walked down a trail that skirted marshy ground and wound through dense and vigorous regrowth. Light showers fell. Back at the hut we packed and chatted with Don. He was reluctant to take to the road and preferred talking to pedalling.

Throughout the morning more campers drove into the campground. Shannon was filling up, and we wanted to be away. Rain or no rain we preferred to be on the track walking in the forest. Waugals pointed the way from the campground to an overgrown and scrubby former logging road along the Shannon River. We were back on the Bibbulmun.

The Shannon River drains karri, jarrah and marri forest that receives between 1000 and 1400 millimetres of rain per year. None of the catchment has been cleared for agriculture, and the river water is fresh and low in nutrients and sediments. After flowing south through steep valleys in its upper reaches, it crosses a wide, swampy coastal plain, turns east and discharges into Broke Inlet, a large estuary of 48 square kilometres.

The river basin supports no agriculture, but much of the area has been logged. Despite the logging, the relatively pristine condition of the river and the associated stands of old-growth karri and some old-growth jarrah had long attracted the attention of conservationists. They organised and agitated to have the area protected. Despite opposition from the

Forests Department, the Shannon River basin was gazetted a national park in 1988. The entire catchment and Broke Inlet are now contained within the contiguous Shannon and D'Entrecasteaux National Parks.

Environmentalists celebrated park status as a great victory. But there can be no unequivocal victories in conservation—only stays of execution. The celebrations were premature, at least partly because environmentalists are trapped in a rhetoric that is itself antithetical to conservation.

The modern environmental movement, characterised by professionalism and bureaucracy, came into existence in the 1960s and 1970s. Previous conservation efforts had emphasised the natural world. The new movement, made up of leftist activists who shared the fashionable social justice concerns of the time, emphasised humans and human welfare. These activists derived their outlook from the socialist crusade to remake the world, to make humans and the world perfect, to enable each and every individual to realise their full potential.

Changes in the conservation movement accompanied changes in language. Conservationists began talking less about people and nature and more about humans and the environment. The new word *environment* was clinical, scientific and, above all, human centred. The new equation banished nature and stressed human welfare.

But there were other reasons why *environment* became popular and *nature* fell out of fashion. Leftists had always been environmentalists. The change in emphasis was on their terms. People on the left held the view that the environment was the major influence on character, both of individuals and of society. As environmentalists they believed that people are formed by their circumstances, that is, by their environment. Moreover, because environments were plastic, humans had the power and obligation to alter them. Change the environment and you change human beings. Improve the environment and you improve human beings, pushing them always towards perfection, without defect of any kind. Environmentalists believed, above all, in the prospects of improvement. They were progressives, and the stories they told about the world were stories of progress.

None of these stories had anything to say in favour of nature. Nature was simply malleable material that existed for human use. Socialists had traditionally no more concern for nature than capitalists. Both socialists and capitalists dreamed of a utopian future when the whole world, the whole environment, would be turned over to humans.

Environmentalism temporarily and artificially united the conservation movement, the peace movement, the social justice movement, the counterculture, the interest in Eastern religions and the concern with health. But it was an unstable and self-contradictory coalition. About the only interest the constituents had in common was an idealisation of the pursuit of self-liberation—the belief that only the self matters. Towards this end, they have been victorious.

With the spread of the global economy and global culture, self-liberation has become the dominant purpose of virtually the entire human population. Self-liberation is publicly endorsed and publicly supported. It operates invariably to the detriment of life on the planet, and it is sanctioned by environmentalism.

In its liberal use of labels, its addiction to slogans, its progressive beliefs and its sponsorship of personal liberation and self-realisation, environmentalism betrays an affinity with the consumerism it claims to repudiate. Yet this connection is hardly recognised. Environmentalists are confused about their own motives. They want to question economic imperatives, but they also want to appear reasonable and professional. And reasonableness and professionalism require environmentalists to adopt the language of their erstwhile opponents and talk about resources, yield, use and distribution. This vocabulary undermines any attempt to question economics. Confused motives and corrupt language produce uncertain results.

Preservation in the guise of environmentalism has failed. Despite decades of hard work by scores of well-meaning people and despite the spectre of sustainable development (actually a code phrase for a fantasy future of spiralling consumption that leaves no ill consequences), the complex and diverse organism of the earth is in steady decline.

Preservation in the guise of environmentalism failed because its strategies and its language reinforced the primacy of exploitation. Environmentalism undermined preservation because it borrowed a progressive model of human society from Adam Smith and a progressive model of nature from the scientific program to conquer the planet. The language of environmentalism disavows the world it means to preserve.

The persistence of the idea of the earth as a resource to be organised for the purpose of human consumption and self-realisation poses great difficulties for nature lovers who wish to tell non-progressive stories about the land and the people on the land. Most people, conditioned by 30 years of environmentalism, invariably identify nature lovers as environmental-ists. Yet the vernacular of environmentalism—resources, management, efficiency, yield, productivity, development—derives from the lexicon of progress and can never provide expression for a view that regards Earth as home, not as habitat, and that views the life in and around us as grace, a gift we have inherited and have done nothing to deserve.

After pushing our way through the overgrown track that followed the Shannon River, Carol and I turned sharply left onto a wide and open road.

The track led away from the river onto a plateau of diverse vegetation. Plants and plant associations changed every few steps: karri forest, karri–marri forest, marri, heathland dominated by tea-trees. Wildflowers were profuse, including many we had not seen before. The morning was cool and overcast. Clouds raced across the sky.

Five kilometres after leaving the Shannon River, we reached a road junction before a bridge over Fish Creek, a tributary of the Shannon. CALM had designated the site 33A. A rock fire ring in the middle of the junction indicated that hikers had camped here before. We pitched the tent in the middle of the crossroads to avoid dangerous karri canopy.

Although we were only a few metres from the creek, a thick, entangling scrub made most of its length inaccessible. A wooden bridge afforded the only access. My foot broke through one of the rotted side planks, and I slid down the bank to the vigorously flowing stream. Although coloured brown with tannin and sharp to the taste, the water was otherwise drinkable.

It was early afternoon. We gathered firewood, lit a fire and boiled water for hot drinks. We cooked pancakes for lunch. Carol reflected on the great distance we had come since Kalamunda—more than 500 kilometres.

During the night the fire burned low, the clouds cleared, filled the sky, cleared and filled the sky again. At the coming of dawn, of rosy-fingered Eos, the sky cleared momentarily. The earth was still. In stillness we were hiking; in stillness we were in the forest.

Modern humanity's attempts to shatter the stillness of the world, to light the darkness of the night, to conquer, control and cover the planet with smoke and steel and concrete, to rise above our animal being and especially our unattainable ambition to live forever, are ugly, intrusive and destructive—and were foretold in the Greek myths.

Eos, the Greek goddess of the dawn, had many lovers. Ganymede, considered the most beautiful youth alive, was her favourite. Zeus, however, desired Ganymede as his own bedfellow. He disguised himself with eagle feathers and abducted Ganymede from Eos. By way of compensation, Eos begged Zeus to confer immortality upon her other lover, Tithonos. Zeus complied.

But in her request for eternal life for her beloved, Eos forgot to include a request for eternal youth. Tithonos became greyer and more wizened every day. Worse, he talked incessantly in an ever shriller voice. Eventually, Eos grew tired of nursing him. Once granted, however, immortality could not be cancelled. Exasperated, Eos transformed Tithonos into a cicada and put him away in a box.

The Greek gods were immortal and powerful, Zeus immensely so, but they were not perfect. Greedy, jealous, temperamental, vengeful and conceited, none was free from moral or metaphysical defect. Nor were they self-created. They were born, even if sometimes by rather unorthodox mechanisms, they could suffer injury, they were not indivisible and they did not possess infinite attributes. Not even Zeus could stand alone in the universe.

Perhaps the Greeks' belief in their gods was superstition, but the modern world has not cleared minds of superstition, error or myth. The present age is, above all, an age of superstition. And some of our shallowest superstitions—like the superstition of Economic Man, the superstition that greater wealth brings greater happiness and the central superstition of science that nature is a machine—have the authorisation of our hardest-headed rationalists and realists. But they are still superstitions.

Take science, wealth and happiness. The powers given to us by science and technology to gratify our needs actually compound and multiply them: as our power increases, our satisfaction diminishes. If happiness is a function of needs in harmony with our capacity to satisfy them, 'progress' will always mean that power, however fast it grows, will be outstripped by needs, which grow faster. The more powerful people become, the more miserable they feel. All that we have only serves to make us need more, and the more we have, the more we need in order to protect what we have.

Modern superstitions, myths and stories have not made the world more safe, more just, more loving or more hopeful than the world constructed by the stories told by our ancestors. Modern progressive stories correlating happiness to greater numbers of people have succeeded in increasing the number of humans; modern progressive stories correlating happiness to wealth have succeeded in increasing the quantity of artefacts on the earth. But neither of these stories nor their consequences have made life or the planet more secure.

Not that the stories traditional people told meant that the tellers were paragons. Outlook, culture and storytelling are important but are not the only defining differences between traditional people and moderns. Numbers are crucial.

In the past the planet survived human depredations not because traditional people instinctively respected life, but because humans could not damage it enough to matter. Traditional people, limited in numbers and means, had no choice but to respect nature, and their stories reflected and maintained that respect. But now there are multitudes of human beings with multitudes of means and multitudes of insatiable appetites, and the damage that we do is systematic and widespread. And our stories celebrate destruction as a triumph of wealth.

At Fish Creek the ashes in our fire were still glowing in the morning. Dry leaves blazed into flame on contact. Carol and I folded the tent, cooked breakfast, crossed the creek and climbed steeply out of the creek's basin. In less than a kilometre we reached Dog Road, our main route for the day.

The weather was alternately sunny and overcast, warm and cool, dry and drizzly. A dying frog lay on the track in the sun. We saw the tail of a snake as it whipped into roadside brush. We passed many side roads named O'Sullivan: O'Sullivan 5, O'Sullivan 12 and plain old O'Sullivan Road. At the end of 15 kilometres, Dog Road came to a junction. To the left the Bibbulmun continued on Marron Road. Straight ahead a track led to Dog Pool, on the Shannon River. A large fallen karri blocked the road. We climbed over the trunk through tangled branches and soon reached Dog Pool, a beautiful place.

The river flowed strongly, rounded a bend, slipped over a slope of smoothed granite, tumbled into Dog Pool, churned up a lather of brown foam and flowed on. Tall trees and medium trees—straight karri, spreading peppermint and wiggly marri—green and enclosing, lined the banks that rose steeply from the water.

Karl Marx, the systematiser of economic thought after Adam Smith, claimed that the water of a waterfall, such as the cascade at Dog Pool, had no value because it had not been produced by labour. His claim betrays the clumsy, imperious conceit of the modern mind, which presupposes that nothing existed before being realised by human thought and labour. For Marx, as for Smith, nature, far from being the generator of all true wealth in society, was a mere abstraction and a limitation on economic progress.

Carol and I thought otherwise. We sat by the river and watched the water make its way. We had arrived early and were in no hurry.

Behind us a stretch of bush along the entrance road had recently burned. Much of the underbrush was dead and provided ample firewood. During our hike through jarrah country, we had lit camp fires only occasionally. But on nearly every night in karri country we had a fire. Nights were dark and damp, and there was an abundance of fallen wood suitable for burning, particularly from karri, which sheds branches profusely. The wood was usually dry, never rotten and burned well.

The sun set. Firelight reflected off the albescent trunks of karri trees as a very dark, cloudy night closed in. But there was no rain, and we fell asleep to the sound of water gurgling over the ledge in the river and to the whisper of a breeze stirring the leaves in the tall karri canopy. Day and night, river running, breeze blowing—the silences and sounds of nature.

Nature, as the Greeks understood it, referred to the earth's ability to come into being and function without human aid. But coming into being did not necessarily imply constant change and dynamism. On the contrary, the most remarkable feature of nature is its stability, its periodicity and cyclicism, its ability to perpetuate and replace itself. This is very different from directional, purposeful, progressive change.[1]

Nature as stable, nature as progressive, are two different views of the world. Both of them are human inventions. The stories they give rise to are not transcripts of nature. Yet these stories, scientific or poetic, do reflect our sense of participation in the world and our perception of reality. And in the human story, in the actual unfolding chronicle of human life on the planet and in the history constructed by historians, that perception of reality becomes a part of the actual reality that people live. Stories have real effects.

Scientific narratives about the world and our place in it are usually based on premises first articulated by Englishman Francis Bacon (1561–1626). Bacon rejected the Greek conception of nature. In particular, he rejected Aristotle's advice that we look on the physical world with wonder, awe and reverence. Bacon did not believe there was something unequivocally right in the natural world, worth preserving, respecting or understanding in itself. Wonder was to cease, to be replaced by use. Use of the world was the human way to fit into the world. Knowledge was not only usefulness but power, a means to thrust human purpose outward and forward into the boundless potential of the future. Only by applying knowledge would humans improve their place in the world. And nature was itself the most fundamental tool.

These premises prejudice outlooks. Most science operates in the context of Baconian purpose—the world exists to be dominated, subdued and conquered. But scientists are creatures of their culture in other ways as well. They are subject to wishful thinking, and they can be bought.

For example, Murray Ryall, in the preface to a compilation of papers presented at a 1992 conference on dieback in Western Australia, profusely thanked Alcoa for its sponsorship and complained: 'Little credit or recognition has been given to the outstanding research contributions and funding by Alcoa and other mining companies.' But perhaps it would not pay to delve too deeply into the reasons for the funding. Most of the research conducted by conference participants depended directly or indirectly on Alcoa funds or other financing from the mining industry. The source of their livelihood determined the questions researchers asked and, most crucially, the questions they did not ask. Not surprisingly, no researcher examined, or questioned, the role of bauxite mining in spreading dieback. Alcoa's money had been well spent.

Ryall dismissed criticism of bauxite mining as 'emotional rhetoric'— as if the mining industry's fervour for profit and growth and scientists' devotion to careers and research funding contain less emotion than a love for the forest. To practise science, to engage in business in the first place, requires desire, an aim already favoured and adapted by our feelings as well as our intellects. Scientists and businesspeople, no matter how hard they might try, cannot avoid feeling.[2]

Emotion and pay-off also play a determining role in the debate over global climate change. Reports of changes in the world's climate have been commonplace for fifteen to twenty years. An understanding of the ill-effects arising from the extravagant burning of oil and coal has been around even longer. Yet governments, corporations and the media are unwilling to hear the message. Resistance is understandable. Energy industries now constitute the largest single enterprise on the planet. Moreover, they are indivisible from automobile, farming, shipping, air freight and banking interests. The oil industry alone has annual sales in excess of one trillion dollars and daily sales of more than two billion dollars.

Over the last five or six years, many of the world's politicians and most of the world's media have promoted the perception that worries about climate are overwrought. In Australia the media columnists who have most assiduously pushed for free markets and free trade—P.P. McGuinness, among others—have also been the most vociferous in denouncing predictions of global warming. Much of the denial has been backed by the energy industry.

In the United States the energy industry has relied on a small band of sceptics—Dr Robert Balling, Dr Pat Michaels, Dr Sherwood Idso, Dr S. Fred Singer and Dr Richard S. Lindzen—who have proved extraordinarily adept at draining the issue of all sense of urgency. Through frequent pronouncements in the press and on radio and television, they have helped to create the illusion that the question of climate change is hopelessly mired in unknowns. But while the doubters portray themselves as besieged truth seekers fending off irresponsible environmental doom-sayers, their testimony is backed by hundreds of thousands of dollars of interested money.[3]

Balling, director of the climatology program at Arizona State University, has received as much as $350 000 from the oil and gas indus-tries and from Kuwait, a leading oil producer. Michaels, a professor at the University of Virginia, who, along with Balling, has testified before Congress in favour of reducing federal financing designed to monitor climate trends, has received more than $200 000 from petroleum and coal interests. Idso, who has worked closely with Balling, has received an undisclosed amount of funds from oil, gas and utility sources. Singer has received consulting fees, amounting to several thousand dollars a day, from Exxon, Shell, Unocal, Arco and Sun Oil.[4]

In Australia identical energy interests exercise a more direct influ-ence over government policy on global warming. During 1997, in forums around the world, the Howard government not only opposed quotas on global greenhouse gas emissions and sought Australian exemption from any internationally agreed targets but specifically argued that Australia be allowed to increase emissions—already among the highest on a per capita basis in the world. Government spokespeople justified the policy on the basis of research conducted by the Australian Bureau of Agricultural and Resource Economics (ABARE).

ABARE's findings, however, were not neutral, nor did they represent a body of objective knowledge. The recommendations had been bought. Parliamentary and other disclosures revealed that energy companies, including Texaco, Mobil, Exxon and BHP, and industry groups, including the Business Council of Australia, the Minerals Council of Australia and the Australian Aluminium Council, had funded ABARE's research, with total contributions of at least $560 000.[5]

Stories have real effects. The stories of denial that bribed scientists, free-market columnists and corrupted governments tell about global warming focus discussion on whether there is a problem in the first place. They have, in effect, silenced debate over what to do about it.

The compromises agreed to by national leaders at the United Nations Climate Summit held in Kyoto, Japan, in December 1997 effectively scuttled meaningful action on greenhouse emissions. The fossil fuel industry succeeded in undermining the political will to agree to a treaty that would limit global warming. Lobbyists, corrupt scientists and columnists drained the issue of all urgency and created enough doubt and uncertainty for politicians to feel that they need not act.

13

Be abundant in love, scant in use

Early in the morning, as the Shannon River glided over granite slabs on its way to Broke Inlet and birds called from high in the karri canopy, Carol and I walked out of Dog Pool camp. At the end of the access road, just before rejoining the Bibbulmun, we clambered over the fallen karri. Perhaps the barrier explained why no one was camping at Dog Pool on this long weekend: it barred vehicular access, and people do not like to wander far from their cars.

We turned right and proceeded southeast, roughly parallel with the Shannon River, along Marron Road. The country was undulating, and we crossed several streams flowing into the Shannon. Vegetation varied: islands of tall karri towered over surrounding heathland. Patches of jarrah–marri and karri–marri forest also stood out among the swampy heath.

After a couple of hours we reached the end of Marron Road at the junction with Pingerup Road, the border between Shannon and

D'Entrecasteaux National Parks. We paused for morning tea and rested by the road. A pig hunter with three leather-padded and muzzled dogs in the back of his pick-up drove by. We turned southwest along Pingerup Road and entered karri country. Many of the stands were virgin: a mixture of old and young, a blend of decay and vigour, a union of broken and whole.

Near the end of Pingerup Road we saw a walker coming towards us, without a pack but carrying a pair of binoculars. We guessed he was a bird watcher. It was so unusual to see someone actually walking in the forest that we stopped in amazement to talk. He was English, touring the southwest to spot birds. He was also interested in wildflowers.

Soon, we passed the bird watcher's vehicle, an old Land Rover, parked at the corner of Pingerup and Chesapeake Roads. Chesapeake Road is a graded, maintained secondary route that runs southeast–northwest, roughly parallel with the coast, and connects Northcliffe and Broke Inlet. We had reached stage 35A. Our map indicated a campsite a kilometre west down Chesapeake Road, where the road crossed the Shannon River. We walked west but the camp proved imaginary.

Chesapeake Road ran along a formation above and across low-lying and watery heathland. At the bridge over the Shannon, swamp spread along both banks of the river. The only dry land was the road and the shoulder. We were not going to camp there. Our map indicated another campsite 2 kilometres back east along Chesapeake Road and 3 or 4 kilometres down a track south across the swamp to the Shannon.

We turned around, passed the Englishman's Land Rover again and reached the junction with Springbreak Road. We turned south, towards the ocean, and stepped around a gate. Most of the day had been overcast but as we started down Springbreak Road, the clouds began to clear. Soon, blue sky extended from horizon to horizon. The track, which cut across peaty swamp and heathland, was flooded in many places. We either walked through the puddles or found a way around. Towards the river the track rose a little. The soil was sandy and drained. We entered timbered bushland. Birds called from the fringing foliage. Scat on the track indicated the presence of dingoes.

The track ended at a small clearing around a large marri tree on the northern bank of the Shannon River. A couple of kilometres east the river entered Broke Inlet. Six kilometres south lay the Southern Ocean. We could hear the roar of the breakers. Carol instantly pronounced the spot superior to camping on the side of Chesapeake Road. She was glad we had made the extra effort.

Our only misgiving was the mosquitoes. They swarmed over us as soon as we stopped, in greater numbers and with greater ferociousness than we had before encountered. Approaching darkness and wood smoke kept them at bay.

At nightfall a flock of yellow-tailed black cockatoos flapped and dived through the air as they fussed about choosing a roost in the dead branches of nearby karris. We kept a small fire burning. Stars appeared and disappeared, obscured and revealed by passing clouds. Away in the bush dingoes howled and whined.

In walking day after day, I have had a chance to make sense of what we have seen. In the compound of sound and silence that pervades the forest I have perceived connections to a series of unique events. I have imposed unifying themes on a flux of diverse and scattered incidents and observations. I have wrung meaning from the world.

Some stories complement other stories; some stories cancel and overwhelm other stories. Syd Shea's story about how wealth justifies destruction extols the story of wealth (economics) and downplays, diminishes and dismisses the story of destruction. Syd Shea will not like my story. In my story wealth creation does not play a central, creative role. In my story wealth creation extirpates life. But that is because my story honours and celebrates life before wealth.

Wealth and destruction, economics and extinction are not unconnected; they belong to the same story. But such an integrated story will not be told by economists or bureaucrats. For the pursuit of wealth generates its own justifications, in particular its own world view, a view that encourages blindness and illusion, that values wealth and discounts destruction.

Economics takes the life out of the world, literally and metaphorically. Market society understands itself—through the ideology of the market—as a self-regulated machine. Economists reduce human life to mechanistic terms, comprehensible through number and calculation.

Economists' assumptions tend to be self-fulfilling. By following their recommendations and establishing an economy—and a polity—predicated on human selfishness, society not only recognises but also encourages a selfish element in our nature.

Once liberated, selfishness, operating in the market, produces rationalisations for its central idea—the indefinite expansion of wealth—and creates and empowers people disposed to voice those rationalisations. Over time, bureaucrats, politicians and foresters tend to become the Economic Man that market theory propounds. They believe that no one can act out of genuine concern or love or selflessness. Every act is an act of self-promotion and economic self-interest. They believe that those who warn about global warming benefit financially from a worried public. And they talk incessantly about the need for a balance between environment and economics. They never talk about the connection between humans and nature.[1]

In 1992 the Western Australian Environmental Protection Authority (EPA) endorsed CALM's latest proposals to maintain woodchipping in the karri forests and to increase the cut from the jarrah forests through clearfelling. The EPA said that CALM had 'the ability, the will and the financial and technical resources to regenerate and manage the State Forest so that it can be harvested in ways which will promote timber growth and supply a technologically advanced timber industry increasingly capable of utilising all the wood produced'.[2]

Environmentalists protested the EPA review. The government appointed another review committee. Headed by Tos Barnett, the new review also endorsed the CALM proposals and concluded that CALM, the EPA and appellants (conservationists and forest industry representatives) were all seeking the same end: 'To strike an appropriate balance between the basic need of the timber industry to fell trees and remove logs and residue from the forests and the need to preserve a healthy forest environment'.[3]

Barnett did not inquire how forest exploitation had become a 'basic need'. His inquiry, like all such inquiries, was self-limiting. The terms of debate were restricted, not only by the bureaucratic and managerial imperatives Barnett was meant to uphold but also by the overarching utilitarianism of the appellants. This enabled Barnett to discern what he called 'a common theme' in their submissions. But the discussion had been framed to find precisely that. The outcome was given at the beginning; the inquiry assumed what needed to be proved. Barnett's formula, 'the appropriate balance', concealed precisely what had to be doubted.

The idea of 'balance' affirms politicians, industry and environmentalists in their necessary delusionary belief that everything that humans find desirable and worthwhile is ultimately connected and compatible. All conflicts are resolvable. Profit, exploitation, growth, community, conservation and happiness can exist simultaneously. It was just a matter of finding, in Barnett's palliative phrase, 'the appropriate balance'.

Barnett also praised the 'good intentions' of all the appellants. But there must be something deeply wrong with good intentions if they all lead to the same destructive end.

Following the Barnett report, a new government appointed another expert committee to review the reviews. Like the previous reviews, this one (the Meagher Report) gave CALM, the government and the timber industry what they wanted—a complete endorsement of the CALM proposals.[4]

All the reviews were alike in their style and their outlook. Their language was uniform—dull, unreflective, passive, often convoluted and without a trace of doubt or critical interest—chosen for its ability to give authenticity and authority to a version of the world that portrays nature as a tool (an environment), extols utility, management, growth and exploitation and tolerates no contradiction.

Tos Barnett and Syd Shea live in and serve a society in the grip of the cult of growth. The obsession to harness ever more resources ever more efficiently to yield ever more production dominates the national discourse. The dogma that greater wealth—whether for an individual or an entire country—implies a greater sense of happiness or wellbeing is so obvious that it requires no demonstration or explanation. The dogma is founded upon illusion, but people fiercely resist disillusionment.

The chief measure of growth of wealth, gross national product (GNP), is a recent invention. Only in the last 50 years have nations boasted of their GNP, or condemned themselves, or been condemned because their per capita growth rate was low. Only in the last 50 years have people come to see themselves as consumers and to expect an endless flow of new types of products. Only in the last 50 years has industry been geared to meet the needs of the affluent society. And more degradation has occurred in Australia in the last 50 years—the years of

GNP worship, high population growth, high economic growth and increasing trade—than in the previous 150 years.

Those who claim that Australians have never had it so good invoke simple-minded arguments. To say that the water is safer to drink and the air is cleaner than 100 years ago displays an unquestioning optimism, a level of emotional shallowness and an intellectual superficiality difficult to sustain, even for economists. What water and what air are they talking about? Australia's optimists could not be talking about the totality of ground water in the country, since the amount that is polluted now is vastly greater than the amount Australian industry and agriculture managed to contaminate a century ago. Nor can they be talking about the condition of the atmosphere over the continent. A century ago the wood fires and furnaces of Australia had barely begun to spew the volumes of particulates and toxins that are now disgorged into the air in countless tonnes.

All this polluting and disgorging augments GNP, an intangible measure that exists only in people's minds. GNP has no life of its own and is simply a way of giving a numerical abbreviation (expressed in dollars) and a positive gloss to a sum of life-destroying activities. The growth of GNP depends on transforming and degrading land, soil, forests, water and air.

But the belief that unlimited economic growth (measured by GNP) can be accomplished within limited space, with limited materials and with limited intelligence only shows the unlimited self-confidence and self-delusion of the people who continue to prescribe growth as a social goal.

Growth depends on and in turn reinforces a culture that grants humans an enormous destructive licence. This licence has been greatly extended over the last several hundred years and has widened even more in the last 50 years. Those who champion that licence—forest managers, loggers, miners, politicians, economists—dismiss scruples about rapine as irrational. It is not always clear, however, exactly how reason conflicts with preservation.

Although each act of plunder—damming a river, logging a forest, mining a hillside, farming arid land—may be rational in a limited, instrumental sense, the overall consequence—degradation and destruction on an unprecedented scale—is disastrous. But even disaster can be made to appear rational when disguised as wealth.

At our camp under the marri tree by the Shannon River, the dingoes were in conversation much of the night, the only sound above the distant surf. When Carol and I woke in the morning, a terrifically loud, full and rich chorus of birdsong surged into our consciousness. We had never heard anything so varied, diverse and continuous. In honour, Carol named the site Splendid Birdsong Camp.

We began walking early, with the birds still in full chorus. We crossed the heath and swamp, its flowers sparkling and glorious in the full sun of morning. A large number of the blossoms were white. The heath family, Epicridaceae, which is highly developed in the southwest with twelve genera, has many white-flowering species. The widespread swamp myrtle (*Homalospermum firmum*), with large white flowers, was in bloom as was the white-flowered shrub *Hypocalymma cordifolium*. But not all was white. Spindle heath (*Cosmelia rubra*), a slender plant that rose above the dense scrub of the swamps, was coming into bloom with drooping, deep red flowers. Small heads of yellow flowers tipped the melaleucas growing on the sandy soils. And on the drier margins, Albany bottlebrush (*Callistemon speciousus*) thrust out bright red brushes of flower.

At Chesapeake Road we turned right and walked southeast along a roadbed straight, wide and flat. We could see a long way ahead. Waugals were infrequent, but there was nowhere else to go. Across the swamp and heath to our right we could see the waters of Broke Inlet and hear the roar of the ocean. The country varied. We passed virgin karri forest containing trees with bifurcated trunks and broken limbs. Jarrah and marri forest stood above the plain of swamp and heath where climbing trigger plant (*Stylidium scandens*), in bloom with pale to deep pink flowers, trailed over small shrubs. A deep blue, far-reaching sky joined one horizon with the other.

After an almost undeviating walk of 11 kilometres we reached the end of Chesapeake Road. We turned right down Broke Inlet Road to Camfield, a squatter settlement on the shore of the inlet. A tiger snake lay coiled in the sun by the side of the road. The settlement was deserted. We dropped our packs and walked along the sandy and rutted foreshore track lined by about two dozen weatherboard and corrugated iron shacks.

Broke Inlet is closed from the sea by a sandbar much of the year. In winter the Shannon River pours enough water into the inlet to break the bar; it then stays open for up to six months. Far across the inlet we could see scrub and sandhills. A very strong sea breeze blew from the south. The few boats floating near a boat launch rocked and strained at their mooring lines. The wind was cold and unpleasant at the water's edge. We returned to our packs and sheltered under a squatter's veranda.

Four men in a four-wheel drive towing a boat pulled up. They were from Perth and had a shack on the other side of the inlet, accessible only by boat. They planned to spend the next few days there fishing but said the forecast was for stormy and rainy weather.

Later, two women in a sedan with Victorian plates drove by. They were touring Western Australia and car camping. They asked us about the shacks. All illegal, in the sense that the owners had no title to the land on which their buildings sat (the land was part of D'Entrecasteaux National Park), but tolerated, we told them. They could camp anywhere they liked. Camping here, however, seemed too much like roughing it and they left.

Light showers overnight turned to a persistent drizzle at dawn. A thick mist obscured Broke Inlet. We packed under the shelter of the veranda. The drizzle turned to a light but incessant rain, and the day became thoroughly wet. The road squelched under our boots. At the junction with South West Highway we rested by a large log bearing an inscription for D'Entrecasteaux National Park. The rain turned to drizzle.

Traffic was continuous in both directions. Campervans and cars towing caravans sped by, enveloped in clouds of spray. Everyone was in a hurry. The automobile has created a world impatient of place. Everyone is anxious to escape one place and speed through the next. Impatience grows with growth.

The cult of growth is indistinguishable from the cult of the free market and from the cult of free trade. The three cults reinforce and ratify one another.

Markets abhor boundaries. Markets recognise only private interests, free trade, convertible currencies, open banking, enforceable contracts and the sovereignty of the laws of production and consumption. Within their expansive and expanding domain the imperatives of getting and spending are superior to local and national customs, superior to local and national laws, superior even to local and national legislatures and courts.

Today the market without boundaries—a truly global market—has triumphed, partly in reality but, more important, as an ideology. Business, business-corrupted governments and business-minded columnists propagandise daily that national boundaries are disappearing—mere old-fashioned obstacles to achieving market share. Citizens, they say, must reject the narrow particularism of place and embrace free and unlimited trade.

Free trade is an unabashed attempt to replace government with economics and to destroy any sort of local self-determination. The effect is to centralise control in the hands of the global corporations best able to profit from a world free of obstructions to international purchasing power. These global corporations cannot value any place because they must be ready at any moment, by the terms of the market, by the terms of wealth and power, to destroy any place.

Those who champion the global economy believe that the deficiencies or needs or wishes of one place may safely be met by the ruination of another place. To manufacture paper in Japan, global corporations clearcut forests in Australia. To make aluminium beverage containers in Europe, global corporations strip mine forests in Australia.

Consider the making of a pencil (perhaps the pencil used in rewriting the drafts and marking the proofs of this book). The wood came from a cedar tree ripped out of the exhausted and abused temperate forests of California or Oregon and shipped overseas. Machines, tended by workers in Japan or China, reduced the tree (transformed into a log) into slender, hexagonal rods with hollow cores. Other workers (not necessarily in Japan or China) inserted the pencil's 'lead', which originated as graphite mined in Sri Lanka. The brass band at the end of the pencil is made from zinc and copper, possibly mined in Australia (or New Guinea or Bougainville), but wherever mined, guaranteed to leave a trail of toxic dumps, contaminated soil and water and disrupted communities. The metal ferrule holds the eraser plug made from rubber and rapeseed oil grown in Indonesia on land cleared of tropical rainforest, which is rapidly being cleared, incinerated and transformed into smoke and pollution.

Thus the global market joins people, materials, exploitation and destruction from all over the planet to make the simple pencil. And we can go to Kmart or Target and buy this device for a mere 25 cents, a price that economists praise as a measure of the market's efficiency. But there is another side to the story. Thanks to free trade, global ruination comes cheaply—and we are all implicated and dependent.

The global economy is an absentee economy. Most people are not using or destroying what they can see. In the instances where people have destroyed what they can see, their global purchasing power helps them destroy somewhere else as well. That is why, under free trade, the people of Newfoundland, having destroyed their local cod fisheries, are still able to buy cod in their local supermarkets. Their purchases now help destroy Russian cod fisheries.

The ideal of the modern corporation is to be, in terms of its own advantage, anywhere and everywhere and, in terms of local accountability, nowhere. To that end, Bunnings, which began as a local, family owned business, has succeeded in recasting itself into a global corporation, organised expressly for the evasion of responsibility, to be able to respond to global demands, and to be prepared to go anywhere and destroy anywhere, to take as much value as it can as cheaply and as quickly as possible.

By 1986, when Bunnings and its subsidiary companies monopolised virtually every aspect of the timber and woodchip industries in Western Australia, the Bunnings family owned just 25 percent of the company. British interests owned another 25 percent. Other major shareholders included Australian Mutual Provident (AMP) Society, Australia and New Zealand (ANZ) Bank and Colonial Mutual Life Assurance Society. As Bunnings grew, ownership became more diffuse and problematic and responsibility less defined.

In 1987 Wesfarmers began a piecemeal takeover of Bunnings and by the end of the year had acquired 19.3 percent of the company. The takeover continued. By the end of 1992 Wesfarmers owned 44.6 percent of Bunnings, acquired a further 22 percent in 1994 and later proceeded to buy the remainder.

Wesfarmers started business in 1914 as the operating arm of a Western Australian farmers' cooperative. In 1984 the 20 500 members voted to corporatise. By 1997 Wesfarmers had become one of Australia's 50 largest companies. The former cooperative owned 52 percent of the stock. Of the next twenty largest shareholders, one held a little more than 3 percent and only six others held more than 1 percent of the stock. They included Westpac, AMP and ANZ.[5]

Alcoa is another absentee landlord with a colonial relationship to Western Australia. Alcoa of Australia is a wholly owned subsidiary of the Aluminum Company of America (ALCOA). Headquartered in Pittsburgh, Pennsylvania, Alcoa (US) is the world's largest aluminium producer. It has 23 business units (subsidiaries) with 170 operating and sales locations in 28 countries. A bank, a mutual fund and an investment group own 22 percent of the company; 83 600 investors own the rest.[6]

From the junction of Broke Inlet Road and South Western Highway the Bibbulmun followed the highway south for a kilometre then turned left into the bush. We entered flat country, a floristic mix of swamp, heath and jarrah woodland. Through the mist and rain we could see rose cone flower (*Isopogon formosus*), with pungent lobes and red and white flower spikes extending from a woolly bract, coming into flower. Synaphea, a small shrub with antlerlike leaves and yellow elongated flower spikes, was also blooming. Along the sandy track tall kangaroo paw (*Anigozanthos flavidus*) showed yellowish green flowers. In the woodland scrub showy flame pea

(*Chorizema reticulatum*) displayed masses of red flowers on bare stems.

Fresh tyre marks on the track indicated the recent passage of a vehicle. At the end of an 18-kilometre hike we reached the Centre Road ford across the Deep River. The river was high and flowing strongly and the ford impassable. The road down to the ford gave access to several picnic tables and fire pits. On the river's bank stood an old, small, one-room wooden forestry hut. It was deserted, but the fire pit outside the door contained hot ashes, and the surrounding ground had been swept. Much of the immediate bush had been recently burned. Rain began shortly after we arrived, and we took shelter in the hut. We decided to stay the night.

We rued the rain because the ford and the flowing water were exciting, and the river's banks, unburned and green, were beautiful. We would have used fine weather to explore the area more fully. Instead, between showers, we pulled dead wood out of the bush and coaxed a new fire in the fire pit. We sat in the doorway of the hut, listened to the river rushing by and watched the rain splatter on the flames of our fire and fall on the charcoal-blackened ground of the burned bush.

Deep River rises about 50 kilometres from the coast and drains mainly jarrah forest, some in quarantined areas and some in Mt Frankland National Park, before meandering across a short coastal plain and emptying into Nornalup Inlet. Because very little of the catchment is cleared, the water is fresh and low in nutrients. Deep River and Shannon River are the southwest's most pristine rivers.

Abounding with life, Deep River is popular with bushwalkers, bird-watchers and canoeists. The Centre Road ford is a favourite spot with locals and tourists for catching marron and picnicking. During the wet afternoon two couples drove down to the ford. The first pair stayed long enough to chat—just checking the place out, they said. The second pair left as soon as they saw that a fire burned in the pit and the hut was occupied.

14

Dream little,
live large

When Carol and I crossed South Western Highway to the Deep River area, we left D'Entrecasteaux National Park and entered state forest. Like all state forest this jarrah bushland was scheduled for destruction.

In 1993 CALM supervised the 'harvest' of 14 290 hectares of jarrah. A total of 4600 hectares was harvested according to 'release of regeneration' methods and 2120 hectares according to 'establishment of regeneration' methods, where, according to CALM:

> the stands are harvested with the object of thinning them. This is achieved either by harvesting in a way that will release existing lignotubers to grow unimpeded into saplings; or, where there are inadequate lignotubers, harvesting to create a shelterwood under which seedlings are established.[1]

CALM's explanation suggested that logging was doing life a favour: the forest was constipated, waiting only for the laxative hand of CALM to free nature.

CALM's gloss on destruction was entirely self-serving and euphemistic. In reality, jarrah forest is logged in one of two ways: heavy selection logging (removal of all salable trees) or clearfelling (felling all but three wildlife 'habitat' trees per hectare). Regeneration consists of poisoning unwanted trees, burning the waste and abandoning the site.

'Harvest', the most severe and violent euphemism, equates trees with crops and distances CALM from its real business: the destruction of native forest and its replacement by plantations. The term *harvesting*, as applied to other living creatures, whether fish, emus, kangaroos or jarrah trees, exposes the meanest, cruelest, most narrow and homocentric of possible human attitudes towards life. The word reveals the pervasive influence of economics in the modern mindset; and of all the areas of human inquiry, economics is the crudest and most obtuse.

The idea of harvesting, backed by an unquestioned belief in economics, lies behind the perennial proposal that the only way to save Australian wildlife is to make it pay, to put a commercial value on tree kangaroos, goannas, emus and parrakeets. But it has been the urge to make the earth pay that is destroying it. To apply solutions inspired by economics to problems caused by economics is like treating an infection with an extract of sewage.

Yet economics continues to claim converts and to instruct. Formerly accused of ignoring the environment, economists now subject the environment to 'environmental economics' or 'green accounting'. This approach ratifies economics and perpetuates the notion that the environment—actually, nature—is nothing more than a collection of products for human use. This absurdly optimistic assumption is like suggesting that gravity exists in order to make it easier for people to sit down.

Economics corrupts. The wisest, the most enlightened exploitation of resources is insufficient, for the simple reason that the concept of exploitation (which lies at the heart of economics) is so false and so limited that in the end it will defeat itself. The earth will have been plundered no matter how scientific and well planned the plundering has been.

Economics rules CALM, an organisation whose managers and senior advisers are dedicated not to protection but to expanding use—preferably in partnership with global corporations. CALM's managers, in fact, act as if they are in the process of a liquidation sale and the forest is going out of business. In 1993 CALM signed agreements with the Albany Plantation Forest Company—a wholly owned Japanese company formed through a partnership between Oji, Japan's biggest pulp and paper manufacturer, and Itochu, the country's biggest trading house—and with Hansol Forest Products of Korea to plant and harvest tens of thousands of hectares of Tasmanian blue gums. CALM also contracted to supply Simcoa Operations Pty Ltd, which operates a silicon plant in Kemerton and is owned by a consortium of banks headed by Chase Manhattan of New York, with up to 150 000 tonnes of green and dry jarrah every year for fifteen years. CALM described the wood, to be added to Simcoa's furnace, as 'forest residue'. In further pursuit of the dream of total use, CALM established a Centre for Bioproduct Development in 1993 to promote the use of native flora for therapeutic and scientific purposes.

There is nothing new in any of these undertakings. Foresters, timber millers and governments in Western Australia have never been passive suppliers to pre-existing markets. Government and industry understand that markets do not spontaneously spring into being. Markets have to be created. From the time of the felling of the first jarrah tree, Western Australian governments and millers have been active, even aggressive, participants in selling the state's forests.

No stars came out during the night Carol and I camped by Deep River. The sky remained opaque as shower after shower passed by. The rain ceased at dawn, and we cooked and ate breakfast outside the hut. We started walking under an overcast sky. The track was wet, and we sloshed through large, shallow puddles. Islands of karri clustered around large granite boulders. Shortly the Bibbulmun split in two. Straight ahead a dry-weather route required a foot crossing of the Deep River. We guessed the crossing was impassable and so turned right, down an alternative route that took us to South Western Highway.

A kilometre or so down the highway, we walked into CALM's Crystal Springs campground. Campers were just emerging from sodden tents pitched under dripping peppermint trees. We ate a large morning snack: with only one more day on the track, we felt free to finish our supplies. After another few kilometres along the highway, the alternative route rejoined the main Bibbulmun track, and we turned into the bush.

A flooded creek flowed over the path. We waded through water up to our knees and emerged on Shedley Drive, a scenic route along the Deep River. The road looked rather rough for tourist cars, especially considering the several large and deep puddles lying across it. But the walk was magnificent: thick stands of broken, gnarly karri towered over dense rainforest understorey. Soon we came to a group of fire-gutted but living tingle trees.

Red tingle (*E. jacksonii*) is one of the most massive trees in Australia. Although not as tall as karri, with a maximum height of 70 metres, red tingle girths are huge, with diameters up to 5 metres. One specimen measured 20 metres in circumference at the base. Although similar to jarrah in appearance, red tingle has browner bark and a denser crown of leaves. Red tingle grows to a great age but is restricted to a few small areas near Walpole that receive as much as 300 millimetres of rainfall during the summer months, with a total of 1200 millimetres per year.

Farther down the track we paused at the Nuyts Wilderness trailhead. A part of Walpole–Nornalup National Park, Nuyts Wilderness is the only declared wilderness area in the entire state of Western Australia. The trail noticeboard warned of snakes and, at the coast, slippery rocks and king waves. Two birdwatchers, who had driven up from the direction we were heading, parked by the noticeboard and walked down the trail. We continued on the Bibbulmun.

Early in the afternoon we came to fenced paddocks, pasture and Tinglewood Lodge. The lodge was once the farmstead of a Swiss family who settled and cleared the surrounding land early in the century. The property remains in the family. We took a room in the motel adjacent to the main lodge, where we were the only guests. On the veranda in front of our room, with views across paddocks down to the Deep River, we cooked most of our remaining food for lunch.

Later we borrowed the lodge's canoe and paddled up the Deep River between banks heavily vegetated with tea-tree, acacia, blackboy, karri and peppermint. We canoed as far as we could against the current, then drifted back to the lodge jetty. We enjoyed the unaccustomed quickness and effortlessness of the movement, propelled not by our legs but by the current. Rain began as we docked. We hurried to the lodge for afternoon tea.

Halley, the Swiss chef, prepared and served the tea. He told us that Charlotte had spent a night in the lodge a few weeks before. Bibbulmun walkers often stayed at Tinglewood, he added. We told him that what we had missed most on the walk was bread. He offered to bake us a loaf for the rest of the trip.

Rain fell throughout the afternoon. We stayed inside, sat in front of the central open fireplace, dried our boots and read. Dinner was served at 6.30 p.m. We had chicken soup, meat loaf with mashed potatoes and vegetables, and an ice cream sundae. Afterwards, Halley presented the loaf of bread he had baked, fresh from the oven and golden brown. It looked delicious.

One other couple, not staying at the lodge, was in the dining room. After dinner we joined them for tea around the fire. They were visiting Western Australia from Sydney and did not like the southwest, which they found boring. They complained about the weather, the lack of shopping opportunities and the paucity of 'decent' restaurants.

Our after-dinner companions were distressed by the lack of choice in the southwest. But what kind of choice were they talking about?

Economists argue that the market 'serves' individuals by empowering them to 'choose'. The choice, however, is always about which items to buy, never about *whether* to buy. The market does not permit a real choice: to choose not to choose; to engage with nature and not with goods. The foreclosing of this choice diminishes the world.

For example, the freedom to choose among scores of automobile brands has been secured by sacrificing the liberty to choose between private and public transportation. More fundamentally, the widespread availability and use of automobiles has undermined stability in favour of mobility.

Mobility conquered space and distance and created a world in which malls, suburbs, highways, traffic jams, noise and pollution became inevitable and omnipresent. This outcome was never the willed choice of some democratic decision-making body—or, for that matter, of individuals who like driving automobiles and choose to buy one. In buying a car, each purchaser has been led, by Adam Smith's invisible hand, to promote an end that was no part of his or her intention. The choice among automobiles offers a superficial expansion of options within a determined frame in return for surrendering the right to determine the frame. It offers the feel of freedom while diminishing the range of options and the power to affect the larger world.

Free trade is even more confining. Free trade creates a situation where people are no longer free not to trade. They become dependent on trade. The more a country engages with the world, the less free it becomes. Not only does it lose the choice not to trade but it forsakes options on how and when and what to trade. The country becomes governed by necessity. Free choice foreclosed is implied by a chorus of free trade advocates who tell Australians they must transform themselves in certain ways, which they then proceed to prescribe. And the reason? We must respond to the challenge posed by competitors.

Most disastrously, by focusing on commodities, humans become callous towards the earth. And this too is an inevitable outcome of market choice. The free market disallows a choice between caring and not caring because caring involves rejecting the commercial values that the free market promotes and thrives on. Caring involves effort and discomfort; buying and selling are predicated on alleviating effort and discomfort. Caring can hardly compete against not caring. Many people have a conspicuous preference for caring, but the market forbids expression of that caring, for to care would undermine the market's central injunction: people must be willing to destroy any place at any time should the market demand and profit dictate.

Thus, what took the urgent press of life millions of years to create, humans have—in the pursuit of comfort, convenience and conquest and propelled by the economics of extravagant consumption—dismantled and brought to the brink of annihilation in a little more than a century.

Our society gave Carol and me the freedom to walk the Bibbulmun and even to solicit and accept lifts on occasion. However, we were not free to walk in undamaged land. We were not free to walk in a bush uncrossed by roads, to ford rivers unblocked by dams and unpolluted by salt and fertiliser or to camp in forest free of disease and clearcuts. One hundred and fifty years of the application of the ruthless logic of economics meant that we were compelled to endure the ugliness and noise of a landscape plundered and distorted by the narrow and uncompromising demands of producing, buying and selling.

We spent five weeks on the Bibbulmun, five weeks walking through the southwest forests. Towards the end Carol asked me for my impressions. The southwest forests, I reflected, are among the most abused forest estates in the English-speaking world. There is hardly a hectare of land between Perth and Walpole that has not been damaged by exploitation. One cannot walk a kilometre along the Bibbulmun without encountering a crossroad or side track, a consequence of the dense interlacing network of access roads that cut up the forest and facilitate its destruction. This is not just the legacy of the past. Destruction continues, aided and abetted by CALM, and much of it in the name of protection, regeneration and sustainability.[2]

One of the penalties of an education in nature, one of the costs of walking through the bush, is the recognition that one must learn to live in a world of wounds. One must accept the tragic necessity of seeing the damage clearly, without excuses, without illusions.

CALM's program for the forest, like the programs of forest services throughout Australia, is contested. But the debate over the forest is confined to wilderness, old growth and native forest. These terms are too restrictive. The preservation of native forest must also include a debate about the future direction of civilisation. The issue could not be more serious. It is a matter of life and death.

Australia is not in dire need of more roads, mines, dams, reservoirs, pipelines, clearcuts, woodchips, trade or people. Nevertheless, these are the needs, and the only needs, provided for by our present politics and economy. We are in dire need of a conversation about the fate of the earth. But unless the language used to debate these needs changes, no review of the nation's cult of growth will be forthcoming. Unless the terms of debate change, unless the language changes from the joyless, mechanistic, utilitarian vocabulary of economics and science to a vocabulary more passionate and more humble, more joyful and more inspired, the conservation of nature is finished.

The present debate over bauxite mining, dieback, water pollution, logging and salinisation is so fragmented that it obscures the connections that tie all Australians to the Palings Road clearcuts or to the Hawke Block. The obfuscation is deliberate. It precludes well-considered, honest responses to the uncomfortable questions that all these acts of devastation raise about desire and complicity, capitalism and modern culture.

The present state of the southwest forests reveals the terrible logic of economics and the full implications of our appetite for paper, for packaging and for wealth. The state of the forests shows that our appetite remains unabated even as free trade conveniently displaces the costs and consequences beyond the conscience.

These costs and consequences will continue to mount unless Australians moderate their desire to possess. But this will happen only if men and women learn to be more sensuous in their attitude to the world, more ready to enjoy the present moment for itself, instead of frenetically seeking the power and security that wealth promises. Only when Australians learn to look sensuously at the continent will they learn to care for it. And not only to look at it, but to touch it, smell it, taste it, drink it, walk it.

The state of the forests in Australia and their continuing decline contradict society's most cherished beliefs: that it is possible to consume immense quantities of raw materials without consequences; that any problem is fixable, given enough goodwill (Barnett's common theme) and technical ingenuity; and that history is necessarily progressive.

This last belief, actually a superstition, is all-powerful. The world is now saturated with the promise of progress, profit and the control of nature. Tens of millions of people in Eastern Europe have joined with tens of millions in the West and hundreds of millions in the newly developing nations in worshipping free markets as the guarantee of progress.

The idea of progress persists because of its powerful appeal to human hopes. The idea resists challenge because it has bequeathed an all-encompassing, homocentric language that informs the way we think about and tell stories about the world. Environmentalism, especially, is instructed by the language of progress, by the linguistic logic of production and consumption.

If the planet is to survive, or rather, if the species whose fate we determine are to survive, then we need stories opposing the idea of progress. We need stories sympathetic to all life, not just human life.

Unfortunately, belief in progress blinds people to a recognition of the destructiveness of civilisation. We live on a dying plant—the consequence of our history. The depletion of ozone, the build-up of greenhouse gases, the poisoning of air, water and soil, the destruction of forests and the mass extinction of species are objective facts. But people respond to these 'facts' subjectively.

To many, the disappearance of wildness, the substitution of the complexity evolved in nature for the simplicities contrived in human culture, causes scant concern. On the contrary, to the unconcerned the magnification of human artifice over the entire surface of the planet requires celebration as evidence of progress and as the culmination of the historically determined human conquest of nature.

To me, the dying matters. Because I care, my task in this story, and in other stories, is to outline the ways that the past contoured the present and will continue to pattern the future. I seek to understand why our pioneers bequeathed us an impoverished land—not, as progressives believe, a land of boundless opportunity.

Carol and I slept poorly at Tinglewood Lodge. After several weeks on a diet of couscous, felafel, vegetable soup and oatmeal, Halley's food gave us indigestion. Heavy rain fell through the night, making the air in the room stuffy. We rose early and left.

The Bibbulmun followed a steep incline from Tinglewood Lodge. At the top of the rise we could see across pasture and forest to the shimmering delta of Deep River and to the choppy waters of Nornalup Inlet. Dark storm clouds hung in the sky. Halley drove by, stopped and offered us a lift to Walpole. No, we said, we had to walk the last section of the Bibbulmun.[3]

The track turned and descended, back towards the river. The bush— jarrah, karri and red tingle growing above a rainforest understorey— closed in. To our right the Deep River, on its final run before entering Nornalup Inlet, broadened and slowed. We came to a swamp thick with swamp bottlebrush (*Beaufortia sparsa*), which, when it blossoms from January to April, displays orange, tassel-like flowerheads. The track turned again, bordered the swamp, left the river and the inlet and climbed through a sandy heath of tea-tree, bottlebrush and paperbark.

On the rise ahead we saw a number of stumpy, gnarled gum trees. In summer, when in bloom, these trees are laden with masses of flowers ranging from orange to deep crimson. This is one of the few places where the red-flowering gum (*E. ficifolia*), common as a street tree but rare in the wild, grows naturally. Here it is a stunted, rough-barked tree, although old stumps indicate the previous presence of large trees. On both sides of the track melaleucas were in blossom, some with small heads of yellow flowers, some with loose spikes of white flowers.

At the top of the rise, near South Western Highway, we took in further views across forest and heath to Nornalup Inlet. We could also see the smaller, abutting Walpole Inlet, which drains into Nornalup Inlet. The vista widened, contracted and widened as we walked. The track then followed the highway for a couple of kilometres.

With the end in sight we felt as though we had been walking forever, that there had never been a time when we had not been walking. We could hardly believe that we would not be walking tomorrow, and the day after that, and the day after that.

Back in the bush, off the highway, the track meandered, bore south, then east, then north, then east again, as if the track designers were reluctant to follow a direct route to Walpole and the Bibbulmun's close. On the final turn east we walked into Walpole, passed the CALM office, crossed South Western Highway and walked into Pioneer Park. We followed the Waugals to the tourist office but could find no official finale or marker. Nevertheless, this was it, the end of the Bibbulmun, 650 kilometres in five weeks and one day. Carol and I hugged and kissed.

Human history, like evolution itself, is contingent. The consequences of any act or decision, even the act of walking and telling this story, are unpredictable. There is no progressive agenda to the human story, and there is no progressive agenda to the Bibbulmun. The idea of progress persists only because we have forgotten more than we have remembered.

Notes

ABBREVIATIONS AND ACRONYMS USED IN NOTES AND BIBLIOGRAPHY

ACF	Australian Conservation Foundation
AGPS	Australian Government Publishing Service
CALM	Department of Conservation and Land Management (Western Australia)
HUP	Harvard University Press
NLA	National Library of Australia
OUP	Oxford University Press
UC	University of California
WAPD	*Western Australian Parliamentary Debates*

CHAPTER 1 — A FIRST STEP BEGINS (pages 1–13)
1   On the Waugal, or *woggal*, see Daisy Bates, *The Native Tribes of Western Australia*, ed. Isobel White, NLA, Canberra, 1985, p. 219.
2   Information on the state of southwest rivers and reservoirs is from G. Olsen and E. Skitmore, *The State of the Rivers of the South West Drainage Division*, Western Australian Water Resources Council, Leederville, 1991.
3   Daisy Bates, *The Native Tribes of Western Australia*, p. 47.

CHAPTER 2 — THROUGH A FOREST UNDONE (pages 14–26)
1   John Ramsden Wollaston, *Wollaston's Albany Journal (1848–1856)*, ed. Percy U. Henn, Peterson Brokenshaw, Perth, 1954, p. 114.
2   Baron Ferdinand von Mueller, *Report on the Forest Resources of Western Australia*, L. Reeve & Co., London, 1879, pp. 2, 27.
3   Malcolm Fraser, *General Information Respecting the Present Condition of the Forests and Timber Trade of the Southern Part of the Colony*, Government Printer, Perth, 1882.
4   *Royal Commission on Forestry: Final Report*, Perth, 1904.
5   *WAPD*, 17 Sept. 1918, p. 343.
6   Besides sources previously quoted, my history of jarrah forest destruction draws on Ian Abbot and Owen Loneragan, *Ecology of Jarrah* (Eucalyptus marginata) *in the*

Northern Jarrah Forest of Western Australia, CALM, Perth, 1986; and B. Dell, J.J. Havel and N. Malajczuk (eds), *The Jarrah Forest: A Complex Mediterranean Ecosystem*, Kluwer Academic Publishers, Dordrecht, The Netherlands, 1989. In fairness to these authors I acknowledge that *destruction* is not the term they use to describe the modern history of the jarrah forest.

7   I draw my argument concerning identity, in part, from Christopher Lasch, *The Minimal Self: Psychic Survival in Troubled Times*, Norton, New York, 1984.

CHAPTER 3 — BY CANKERED SOIL AND STRANGLED TREES (pages 27–40)

1   J. Ednie-Brown, *The Forests of Western Australia and Their Development*, 2d ed., Government Printer, Perth, 1899, p. 10.

2   Lane-Poole quoted in Athol Meyer, *The Foresters*, Institute of Foresters of Australia, Hobart, 1985.

3   Quoted in Sir James Barrett (ed.), *Save Australia: A Plea for the Right Use of Our Flora and Fauna*, Macmillan, London, 1925, p. 59.

4   Development figures from T.N. Stoate, *Forestry and Forest Resources, Western Australia: Statement Prepared for the Fifth British Empire Forestry Conference (London)*, 1947, Perth, 1947.

5   Linguistic determinism (the idea that language determines the way we think) and linguistic relativism (the idea that distinctions encoded into one language are not found in any other language and thus differences among languages cause differences in the thoughts of their speakers) are fashionable absurdities. Social constructivists and post-modernists invoke them so as to exempt the mind from the fate of Darwinian evolution. However, their plea for human uniqueness is specious. The fact that all human languages differentiate animals, plants, forests, trees, grasses, soil and fire provides telling evidence of the reality of such things. These categories correspond to invariable aspects of the world. They are not arbitrary, socially constructed features but concur with the way the world actually is.

Post-modernists deny these connections. They reject the ideas of biological endowment and of physical reality because, as intellectual libertarians, they are, or want to become, ideological and social managers, seeking to serve or assume power. For people committed to control and manipulation, it is very useful to think that humans have no intrinsic (that is, innate) moral and intellectual character, that nature has no independent existence or worth (it is merely a human construction), and that humans and nature are simply objects to be shaped for their own good. Furthermore, if humans are products of their circumstances and socially created, then they are reinventable according to the dictates of the powerful and those who serve them.

6 My account of dieback partly draws on *Dieback: What Is the Future?* Papers presented at a seminar in Perth, 23 September 1992; The Northern Sandplains Dieback Working Party, Muchea, WA, 1992, and B.L. Shearer and J.T. Tippett, *Jarrah Dieback: The Dynamics and Management of* Phytophthora cinnamomi *in the Jarrah* (Eucalyptus marginata) *Forest of Southwestern Australia*, CALM, Como, 1989. Readers should note that discussion of dieback in these sources may be constrained by the authors' sponsoring organisations.

CHAPTER 4 — TILL EARTH IS AS BARREN AS THE MOON (pages 41–53)
1 *WAPD*, vol. 158, 5 Sept. 1961, p. 741.
2 Quote from *Bauxite Mining in the Jarrah Forest: Impact and Rehabilitation*, a report by the Steering Committee for Research on Land Use and Water Supply, CALM, Perth, 1984. Other information on bauxite mining from *Bauxite: A Report on Bauxite Mining in the Darling Range*, Institute of Foresters of Australia, Western Australian Division, 1980, and Basil Schur, *Jarrah Forest or Bauxite Dollars? A Critique of Bauxite Mine Rehabilitation in the Jarrah Forests of Southwestern Australia*, Campaign to Save Native Forests (WA), Perth, 1985.
3 The above passages draw on the discussion of light and noise in Laurens Van der Post, *About Blady: A Pattern out of Time*, Harcourt Brace Jovanovich, San Diego, Cal., 1993.
4 CALM quote from *Bauxite Mining*, p. 37. Carbon quoted in Schur, *Jarrah Forest*, p. 16. Carbon's prediction may be correct and the outcome catastrophic for reasons beyond his own understanding. Many scientists view nature and the southwest forests as a machine. A machine consists of comprehensible and replaceable parts and operates according to rules and laws that permit prediction. The machine functions in an idealised universe without chance. It has no history: how it will be tomorrow can be predicted from how it is today; there is no need to know how it was yesterday, since that information is observable in its condition today.

The mechanical view implies that nature can be re-engineered; it can be tinkered with and improved upon without ill effect. The mechanical view is, however, inadequate and does not even begin to explain the consequences of intervention.

Characterised by chance and randomness, nature is more like the weather than a machine. Small, chance events at one point in the atmosphere may induce major overall change. Similarly, the life of the forest can depend on irregularities. Human-created disturbances such as dieback and bauxite mining introduce major and far-reaching instabilities. To assume that the consequent change will not be harmful—will, in fact, be beneficial—is the height of folly.
5 My argument concerning the speciousness of the idea of 'a challenge' draws on Edward Abbey, *One Life at a Time, Please*, Henry Holt, New York, 1988.

CHAPTER 5 — WRITTEN IN WATER (pages 53–65)

1   See *Dieback: What Is the Future?* and Angela Wardell-Johnson and Mary Frith, eds, *The Jarrah Book: Proceedings of a Weekend Workshop at Perup Field Studies Centre*, 1992.

CHAPTER 6 — WEALTH WITHOUT LIFE (pages 66–78)

1   The disappearing cod reported by Debora Mackenzie, *New Scientist*, 16 Sept. 1995, pp. 24–29.

2   In the United States the Multiple Use and Sustained Yield Act, passed by Congress in 1960, led to the wholesale dismantling of forests in parts of the west and northwest.

3   Quote from *Bauxite Mining in the Jarrah Forest: Impact and Rehabilitation*, a report by the Steering Committee for Research on Land Use and Water Supply, CALM, Perth, 1984.

4   Quotes from *Land Use Management Plan, Northern Jarrah Forest Management Priority Areas*, Forests Department, Perth, 1980.

5   The government review quoted in Western Australian Forest Alliance, *Analysis of the report by the expert scientific and administrative committee ('the Meagher Report') and the statement of the Minister for the Environment ('the Minson statement') of 5 August 1993*, Perth, Sept. 1993.

6   The United States history of these terms can be found in Paul W. Hirt, *A Conspiracy of Optimism: Management of the National Forests since World War Two*, University of Nebraska Press, Lincoln, 1994.

7   Dr Syd Shea, 'The Middle River Forestry/Conservation Reserves/Recreation Planning', in *Blackwood Conference: Proceedings of a Conference Held at Bridgetown, WA, on Saturday, February 17, 1990*, South West Development Authority, Manjimup, WA, 1990, p. 11.

8   CALM quote from *Bauxite Mining in the Jarrah Forest*, p. 2.

CHAPTER 7 — AN ILLUSION, A SHADOW, A STORY (pages 79–90)

1   For the history of scientific support for increased population in Australia, see William J. Lines, *False Economy: Australia in the Twentieth Century*, Fremantle Arts Centre Press, Fremantle, WA, 1998.

2   For a refutation of the presence of progress in evolution see Stephen Jay Gould, *Full House: The Spread of Excellence from Plato to Darwin*, Harmony Books, New York, 1996.

3   Ian Clunies Ross, *Memoirs and Papers, with Some Fragments of Autobiography*, OUP, Melbourne, 1961, p. 237.

CHAPTER 8 — CHANGES AS THE FOREST IS CHANGED (pages 91–102)

1   The deft phrase 'conspiracy of optimism' comes from Hirt, *Conspiracy of Optimism*.

2   Quoted in R. and V. Routley, *The Fight for the Forests*, 2d ed., Research School of Sciences, Australian National University, Canberra, 1974, p. 18.

3   The story of woodchipping from Mark Streeting and David Imber, *The Price of Australian Woodchip Exports*, Resource Assessment Commission, Research Paper No. 4, AGPS, Canberra, 1991; *The Great Forest Sell-Out: The Case against the Woodchip Export Industry—An Australian Conservation Foundation Viewpoint*, ACF, Melbourne, 1976; Terry S. Walter, *Some Cost-Benefit Aspects of Wood Chipping in Western Australia*, South-West Forests Defence Foundation, Nedlands, 1976; *Karri Forest Facts: Facts and Figures about Western Australia's Karri Forest*, South-West Forests Defence Foundation, Nedlands, 1986; and John Dargavel, *Fashioning Australia's Forests*, OUP, Melbourne, 1995.

4   CALM's preference for plantations over forest betrays the influence of a very ancient philosophy. Most foresters are Platonists. Plato held that actual organisms are only shadows on the cave's wall (empirical nature) and that an ideal realm of essences must exist to cast the shadows. This gave rise to the view that populations of actual individuals (such as the trees in a forest) form a set of accidents, a collection of flawed examples, each necessarily imperfect and capable only of approaching the ideal to a certain extent. CALM foresters have a Platonic view of the jarrah and karri forests. Clearcutting, they believe, will help the forest achieve its true (Platonic) essence. They regard existing variation in the forest (diversity) as imperfect, a consequence of inconsequential happenstance.

5   For an example of faith in management see P.E.S. Christensen, *The Karri Forest: Its Conservation Significance and Management*, CALM, Perth, 1992. For an exposé of CALM's rationalisations for forest destruction see M.C. Calver, R.J. Hobbs, P. Horwitz and A.R. Main, 'Science, principles and forest management: A response to Abbott and Christensen', *Australian Forestry*, vol. 59, no. 4 (1996), pp. 1–6.

The reply to this criticism, 'Objective knowledge, ideology and the forests of Western Australia', *Australian Forestry*, vol. 59, no. 4 (1996), pp. 206–12, by Ian Abbott and Per Christensen, claims the existence of 'a considerable body of objective knowledge upon which forest management is based'. Not only does this assertion beg the question of what constitutes objectivity, but it also assumes what it needs to prove. The authors' undertaking—the establishment of 'objective facts'—is flawed and based on a misreading of science. Objectivity is not absolute but depends on looking at a situation from as many points of view as possible. These points of view are socially given. Knowledge, like truth, depends on socially accepted understanding. It is secure to the extent that human understanding can be secure, but it is always subject to revision.

For these reasons, Abbott and Christensen are bound to be forever embroiled in controversy. Proclamations of 'objective knowledge' invite and demand the most searching inquiry, particularly when they serve political ends, such as the basis of advice to government, as they do in the case of Abbott and Christensen.

CHAPTER 9 — ACCORDING TO THE GOSPEL OF GETTING ON (pages 103–115)

1   Adam Smith, *An Inquiry into the Nature and Causes of the Wealth of Nations*, Modern Library, New York, 1937, p. 423.

2   The idea of the Sovereign Individual is another facile notion popular among economists and economically inclined political scientists. Practically synonymous with the concept of Economic Man and borrowed, in ignorance, from Enlightenment thinkers, the idea is absurd. The truly sovereign individual would be mute, solitary, naked and hungry. Although some people are hungry, others naked, others friendless and still others unable to speak, it is highly unlikely that anyone, anywhere, suffers continuously and simultaneously from all four conditions. The Sovereign Individual does not and cannot exist.

Everything that makes us human and keeps us civilised, every skill that enables us to make our way in the world, from acquiring language to eating, is social in nature. Without reciprocal relations with fellow human beings, a single individual is bereft.

The only people able to become individuals are those in contact with other people and who, through socialisation, learn a language, the difference between right and wrong and so on. It is impossible to conceive of individuals abstracted from their social relations. Society precedes individuals.

Economists, however, assume that life is essentially a struggle against others for survival. This assumption—convenient for people of wealth and power—implies there cannot be any systematic despoliation of the natural world. There can be only more or less efficient control of nature (determined by competition). There can be no overall problem but only separate, isolated problems that can be treated independently of one another. Moreover, problems assume significance only when they affect economic interests.

3   Economic explanations of behaviour are not only inadequate, they are downright misleading. In taking economics and economists seriously, conservationists not only ratify an economic world view but also help license obfuscation and deception.

For example, forest services throughout the world persist in preparing forests for logging that, by strict economic criteria, is uneconomic: destructive, unsustainable and requiring massive public subsidy. These practices are pursued and justified despite the existence of alternatives—such as conservation for tourism—that would generate higher economic returns. And this is precisely where economics is blind. Critics, misinformed by economics, cannot see that forest services, and their governments, function to conquer nature, build empires and proclaim human sovereignty. These motivations lie outside economic reckoning and have little to do with economics. Money serves only as a means to their end, not as the end itself. Economic interpretations of forest abuse fail to recognise these real motivations, and, at the same time, they obscure them.

4   The relationship between emotion and reason is explored in Antonio R. Damasio, *Descartes' Error: Emotion, Reason, and the Human Brain*, Putnam, New York, 1994.

5   I made the connection between economics and autism while reading Oliver Sacks, *An Anthropologist on Mars: Seven Paradoxical Tales*, Knopf, New York, 1995.

6   Christensen, *Karri Forest*, p. 79.

7   On the human mind as a categorising device see Stephen Jay Gould, 'The late birth of a flat earth', in his *Dinosaur in a Haystack: Reflections in Natural History*, Harmony Books, New York, 1995.

8   My argument concerning Luddism draws on Wendell Berry, *Sex, Economy, Freedom and Community*, Pantheon, New York, 1993, pp. 130–31, and on Kirkpatrick Sale, *Rebels Against the Future: The Luddites and Their War on the Industrial Revolution: Lessons for the Computer Age*, Addison-Wesley, Reading, Mass., 1995.

CHAPTER 10 — MONEY ANSWERETH ALL (pages 116–129)

1   Logging figures from *Annual Report, July 1993 to June 1994*, Department of Conservation and Land Management, Perth, 1994.

2   In 1994 CALM announced a roading and logging timetable for the Hawke Block. Later in the year the federal government banned woodchip exports from High Conservation Value Old Growth Forests, including the Hawke Block. CALM, however, remains committed to the destruction of the Hawke Block. At present (1997) this ban is under review and is contested by the Western Australian government. I am grateful to Andy Russell of WEG for this information.

3   The identical nature of the submissions noted by Tos Barnett, *Report to Hon. Jim McGinty, MLA, Minister for the Environment*, Perth, Dec. 1992.

4   Incoherence typifies environmentalist thinking on this matter. An academic correspondent writes: 'The only hope of accomplishing [conservation] is to convince people that there is something in it for them; that the long-term interests

of *homo sapiens* are intimately bound up with the survival of other species.'

Unfortunately for my correspondent's hopes, there is no evidence for any coincidence between the consolidation of human interests—however they may be defined, but particularly in the sense understood by the modern world—and the preservation of species. On the contrary, human prosperity proceeds on the basis of the diminishment and extinction of other species. In any case, where not dangerous or inconvenient, much of nature is useless to human purpose.

In fact, harmony between human interests and preservation could exist only if the earth had been made for humans. This arrogant claim derives from wishful thinking, to which all of us are prone. Promoting self-interest as the incentive for conservation merely perpetuates destruction, since the promulgation of human interests lies behind the conquest of nature in the first place.

My correspondent contradicts herself. She precedes her advocacy of self-interest with the muddled assertion that '[Conservation] requires humans to take themselves out of the centre of the picture, and to view themselves as just one species among many others, each of which is just as important as themselves.' Humility and renunciation are hardly consistent with the idea of promoting conservation on the promise that people will find 'something in it for them'.

CHAPTER 11 — THINGS HOLY, PROFANE, CLEAN, OBSCENE, GRAVE AND LIGHT (pages 130–142)

1   Most economics textbooks cite this domestic etymology to lull students into thinking that the subject is benign and unexceptional. Authors then introduce the less benign but central assumption of economics, rationality.

Despite the well-chronicled human proclivity for logical inconsistency, self-delusion and self-destruction (qualities placed on record in this book), economists insist that humans are rational: people understand where their best interests lie and use reason to pursue them. 'Best interests' is narrowly defined. Individuals make choices in order to maximise their utility—meaning they try to derive as much satisfaction as possible from their actions.

However, even if we ignore the question of whether defining self-interest as individual and never collective adequately describes human psychology, there is a great doubt about the assertion that humans know their best interests. The growing and pervasive presence of therapists, career counsellors, financial advisers, management consultants and advice columnists contradicts the assumption of rationality. Rather, the evidence suggests that most people are confused about where their best interests lie and how to pursue them—that is why they seek help from professionals.

Note, however, that the experts (and politicians), under the sway of market ideology, frame choice in a way that determines which alternatives their clients (electors) choose. The choices are deliberately restricted and reflect the belief that people are economically self-interested—the very assumption in need of proof.

No doubt biologically and, to an extent, socially, humans are self-interested creatures. But interest in self-preservation is not the same as economic self-interest—a very narrow and particular form of self-interest. In fact, the pursuit of individual economic self-interest will just as likely undermine self-preservation as further it—more evidence of the lack of rationality behind much human behaviour.

2   Haeckel saw himself as the founder of a new 'scientific religion'. He called his philosophy monism and hoped to lead a movement of aggressive rationalism that would rid Germany of the last traces of superstitious religion and replace Christianity with a 'religion' that glorified modern science. See Daniel Gasman, *The Scientific Origins of National Socialism: Social Darwinism in Ernst Haeckel and the German Monist League*, Macdonald, London, 1971.

3   Christensen, *Karri Forest*, pp. 61–62.

4   Quote from Edward Shann, 'Group settlement of migrants in Western Australia', *Economic Record*, vol. 1, no. 1, Nov. 1925.

5   Saint-Hilaire and Lamarck quoted in Ernst Mayr, *The Growth of Biological Thought: Diversity, Evolution, and Inheritance*, HUP, Cambridge, Mass., 1982, p. 362.

6   Imberger quoted in 'International demand for UWA researchers', *Uniview Magazine*, vol. 16, no. 3. Oct. 1997, pp. 9–11.

CHAPTER 12 — COUNTENANCE SILENCE (pages 143–157)

1   Natural selection can and does act just as vigorously to maintain stability, or stasis, as it does to bring about change. If certain patterns of life successfully reproduce, they persist. Variations are liable to be worse, and natural selection will therefore tend to eliminate deviants.

2   For Ryall quote see *Dieback: What Is the Future?* Schur, in *Jarrah Forest*, gives further specific examples of research corrupted by mining funding and examines how, either in the pay of mining companies or under the supervision of government, environmental scientists develop ecological and ideological justifications for access to mineral ore by global corporations.

3   My argument concerning the critics of global warming draws on Ross Gelbspan, 'The heat is on: The warming of the world's climate sparks a blaze of denial', *Harpers*, Dec. 1995.

4   These are US dollar amounts, from documents released by Ozone Action

(a Washington group that lobbies on issues of air quality and global climate change) and reported in the *San Francisco Chronicle*, 21 Mar. 1996, 'Critics of warming theory accused', p. A5.

Global warming will not necessarily result in uniform increased temperatures. Warming could just as easily trigger an ice age. The earth's climate is periodic. It oscillates between two poles or attractors: mild and ice age. Global warming increases the temperature a few degrees and moves the mild attractor a little. Ice ages take climate to a totally different attractor, colder by many degrees. We are currently on the mild attractor, but in the space of the possible lurks an ice age.

Disturbances—including filling the atmosphere with carbon dioxide and methane and inducing greenhouse warming—could switch the climate to the cold attractor. It has happened before, in the recent geological past. Rises in temperature have been quickly overcome by general freezing.

5   From information disclosed to the Australian Conservation Foundation (ACF) by Brian Fisher, executive director of ABARE, in letters dated 5 and 9 May 1997. ACF executive director Jim Downey said that the involvement of the fossil fuel industry 'verged on privately funded research buying government policy', *Weekend Australian*, 14–15 June 1997, p. 4.

CHAPTER 13 — BE ABUNDANT IN LOVE, SCANT IN USE (pages 158–171)

1   With respect to the limits imposed on understanding by the idea of Economic Man, consider Shakespeare. Of the hundreds of characters in his plays, few, if any, are motivated by economic self-interest. Even Shylock possesses a complexity that defies economic analysis. Shakespeare presents a universe of humanity animated by power, revenge, jealousy, love, sex, ideals, morality, pride, honour, loyalty, friendship, even stupidity, but rarely economic self-interest. Nothing could be more different from the world portrayed by modern economics.

Accordingly, Shakespeare has been disappearing from school curricula throughout the English-speaking world in direct proportion to which market values insinuate themselves into education. Those educators sensitive only to economic imperatives consider his plays irrelevant. 'Irrelevant' is a code word for subversive. Anything that might give students a deep, tragic or varied point of view challenges the ascendancy of economic thought. Shakespeare's characters do not suit the modern penchant for simple, optimistic, economically motivated ciphers. His plays have been replaced by the multicultural whinging (little more than a demand for equal access to consumer goods) of post-colonial literature.

2   Environmental Protection Authority, *Bulletin 652*, *Proposals to Amend the 1987 Forest*

Management Plans and Timber Strategy and Proposals to Meet Environmental Conditions on the Regional Plans and the WACAP ERMP, Perth, 1992.

3   Barnett, *Report*, p. 13.
4   See Western Australian Forest Alliance, *Analysis*.
5   Information on Bunnings and Wesfarmers from Kevin P. Smith, *A Bunch of Pirates: The Story of a Farmer Co-operative: Wesfarmers*, Westralian Farmers Co-operative, Perth, c. 1984, and from *Australian Public Companies Guide*, Edition 22, November 1996–March 1997, pp. 681–82.
6   Information on Alcoa from *The Value Line Investment Survey*, New York, 2 Aug. 1996, Metal and Mining Industry, p. 1220.

CHAPTER 14 — DREAM LITTLE, LIVE LARGE (pages 172–183)
1   Figures and quotes from *Annual Report, July 1993 to June 1994*, Department of Conservation and Land Management, Perth, 1994.
2   Taxpayers subsidise this destruction. The timber industry pays royalties that fall far short of the amount the state spends on preparing the forest for logging. This deficit represents a substantial taxpayer-funded subsidy to the timber industry. The creation of CALM in 1985 merged the budgets for forestry, conservation and parks and made it impossible to isolate the finances of the state forest service. Amalgamation was thus a neat way of disguising corporate welfare.
3   The Bibbulmun track that Carol and I walked no longer exists. Starting in October 1993, CALM began a complete realignment, which, when complete in August 1998, will retain barely 10 percent of the pre-1993 route. The new purpose-built track shifts much of the route east and places most of it in conservation areas. The realignment includes a south coast extension, some 180 kilometres farther east of Walpole, to Albany.

   At a cost of some $5 million, which includes a federal grant, CALM money and funds from Alcoa, Worsley Aluminium and other corporate sponsors, the new Bibbulmun track features 46 campsites, placed 10–20 kilometres apart and containing shelters, rainwater tanks, picnic tables, toilets and concrete barbecue pits.

Select bibliography

Abbey, Edward, *One Life at a Time, Please*, Henry Holt, New York, 1988.

Barber, Benjamin R., *Jihad vs McWorld*, Times Books, New York, 1995.

Berry, Wendell, *Another Turn of the Crank: Essays*, Counterpoint, Washington, D.C., 1995.

____, *Sex, Economy, Freedom and Community*, Pantheon, New York, 1993.

Botkin, Daniel B., *Discordant Harmonies: A New Ecology for the Twenty-first Century*, OUP, New York, 1990.

Calasso, Roberto, *The Ruin of Kasch*, trans. William Weaver and Stephen Sartarelli, HUP, Cambridge, Mass., 1994.

The Case against Free Trade: GATT, NAFTA, and the Globalization of Corporate Power, Earth Island Press/North Atlantic Books, San Francisco, 1993.

Casti, John L., *Complexification: Explaining a Paradoxical World through the Science of Surprise*, HarperPerennial, New York, 1995.

____, *Paradigms Lost: Images of Man in the Mirror of Science*, William Morrow, New York, 1989.

Cohen, Jack and Ian Stewart, *The Collapse of Chaos: Discovering Simplicity in a Complex World*, Penguin, New York, 1995.

Damasio, Antonio R., *Descartes' Error: Emotion, Reason, and the Human Brain*, Putnam, New York, 1994.

Diamond, Jared, *The Third Chimpanzee: The Evolution and Future of the Human Animal*, HarperCollins, New York, 1992.

Feyerabend, Paul, *Killing Time: The Autobiography of Paul Feyerabend*, University of Chicago Press, Chicago, 1995.

Gare, Arran, *Nihilism Incorporated: European Civilization and Environmental Destruction*, Eco-logical Press, Bungendore, New South Wales, 1993.

Gould, Stephen Jay, *Full House: The Spread of Excellence from Plato to Darwin*, Harmony Books, New York, 1996.

Hammond, J.E., *Winjan's People: The Story of the South-West Australian Aborigines*, ed. Paul Hasluck, Imperial Printing Co., Perth, 1934.

Harte, John, *The Green Fuse: An Ecological Odyssey*, UC Press, Berkeley, 1993.

Hillel, Daniel J., *Out of the Earth: Civilization and the Life of the Soil*, Free Press, New York, 1991.

Hirt, Paul W., *A Conspiracy of Optimism: Management of the National Forests since World War Two*, University of Nebraska Press, Lincoln, 1994.

Lasch, Christopher, *The Minimal Self: Psychic Survival in Troubled Times*, Norton, New York, 1984.

Lears, Jackson, *Fables of Abundance: A Cultural History of Advertising in America*, Basic Books, New York, 1994.

Mayr, Ernst, *The Growth of Biological Thought: Diversity, Evolution, and Inheritance*, HUP, Cambridge, Mass., 1982.

Midgley, Mary, *Science As Salvation: A Modern Myth and Its Meaning*, Routledge, London, 1992.

Pagels, Heinz R., *The Cosmic Code: Quantum Physics As the Language of Nature*, Simon and Schuster, New York, 1982.

Passmore, John, *The Perfectibility of Man*, Scribner's, New York, 1970.

Pinker, Steven, *The Language Instinct*, William Morrow, New York, 1994.

Rothenberg, David, *Hand's End: Technology and the Limits of Nature*, UC Press, Berkeley, 1993.

Sacks, Oliver, *An Anthropologist on Mars: Seven Paradoxical Tales*, Knopf, New York, 1995.

Sale, Kirkpatrick, *Human Scale*, Coward, McCann & Geoghegan, New York, 1980.

____, *Rebels against the Future: The Luddites and Their War on the Industrial Revolution: Lessons for the Computer Age*, Addison-Wesley, Reading, Mass., 1995.

Schmookler, Andrew Bard, *The Illusion of Choice: How the Market Economy Shapes Our Destiny*, State University of New York Press, Albany, 1993.

Smith, John Maynard, *Did Darwin Get It Right? Essays on Games, Sex, and Evolution*, Penguin, London, 1988.

Taylor, Jan, *Australia's Southwest and Our Future*, Kangaroo Press, Kenthurst, New South Wales, 1990.

Thoreau, Henry David, *Walden; or, Life in the Woods*, Holt, Rinehart and Winston, New York, 1948.

Tudge, Colin, *The Engineer in the Garden: Genes and Genetics: From the Idea of Heredity to the Creation of Life*, Jonathan Cape, London, 1993.

Wolpert, Lewis, *The Unnatural Nature of Science*, Faber and Faber, London, 1992.

Index